From Word to Book

From Word to Book

Ten Questions about How We Got the Bible

NANCY R. HEISEY

WIPF & STOCK · Eugene, Oregon

FROM WORD TO BOOK
Ten Questions about How We Got the Bible

Copyright © 2024 Nancy R. Heisey. All rights reserved. Except for brief quotations in critical publications or reviews, no part of this book may be reproduced in any manner without prior written permission from the publisher. Write: Permissions, Wipf and Stock Publishers, 199 W. 8th Ave., Suite 3, Eugene, OR 97401.

Wipf & Stock
An Imprint of Wipf and Stock Publishers
199 W. 8th Ave., Suite 3
Eugene, OR 97401

www.wipfandstock.com

PAPERBACK ISBN: 978-1-6667-8871-6
HARDCOVER ISBN: 978-1-6667-8872-3
EBOOK ISBN: 978-1-6667-8873-0

03/15/24

Scripture quotations except where otherwise noted are from New Revised Standard Version Bible, copyright © 1989 National Council of the Churches of Christ in the United States of America. Used by permission. All rights reserved worldwide.

Quotations marked NETS are taken from *A New English Translation of the Septuagint,* © 2007 by the International Organization for Septuagint and Cognate Studies, Inc. Used by permission of Oxford University Press. All rights reserved.

For Ruth and for Matthew

Contents

Acknowledgments | ix

Introduction | xi

Chapter 1: What Does It Mean to Read the Bible in Translation? | 1

Chapter 2: How Did Ancient Stories Become Hebrew Scrolls? | 14

Chapter 3: How Do Archeological Findings Enhance the Bible's Backstory? | 24

Chapter 4: How Did the Scattering of the People of Israel and Judah Shape the Story? | 35

Chapter 5: How Did Jesus and His Community Enter the Story? | 44

Chapter 6: What Are Biblical Canons, and How Were They Formed? | 59

Chapter 7: How Did the Bible in Spanish Develop? | 72

Chapter 8: How Did Medieval and Reforming Readers Interpret the Bible? | 84

Chapter 9: How Have Modern Discoveries Impacted Understandings of the Bible? | 95

Chapter 10: How Does the Bible Still Speak, and to Whom? | 110

Appendix A: Glossary | 127

Appendix B: Ancient History Comparative Dates | 133

Appendix C: New Testament Manuscripts Overview | 135

Appendix D: For Further Reading | 137

Bibliography | 141

Acknowledgments

First of all, I extend my gratitude to the unnamed storytellers, poets, copyists, paper and ink makers, translators, and editors; to the Bible women who peddled out of their rucksacks, and across the millennia, to all those who sang and prayed the words of Scripture at home, in the dock, and as they traveled. Their patience and commitment brought God's story to the world and to me. As a member of this cloud of witnesses, I name Faye Edgerton, early translator of the Navajo Bible, whose presence in my childhood planted the seeds of this book.

I would not have delved so deeply into the questions considered here without students from two decades of my History of the Bible classes. Special thanks to Mary Harnish and Laurence Sauder, who demonstrated that exploring that history sparks interest across the generations. Thanks to the members of Springs, Pennsylvania, Mennonite Church, and to the Sinapi (mustard seed) Sunday school class at Harrisonburg Mennonite Church, who invited me to share much of this material with them. Special gratitude to the spring 2024 History of the Bible class members for working through all this stuff one more time.

Throughout my teaching career, colleagues and friends Peter Dula, Andrea Dalton Saner, and Carmen Schrock-Hurst kept assuring me that these questions mattered in their work, and recommended me for release time to begin serious writing. Thanks to the faculty scholarship committee at EMU, who granted that release time in 2020. Thanks also to Jason Gerlach, MJ Heisey, Phil Horst, Phyllis Horst Nofziger, Darlene Keller, Wendell Shenk, David Stenson, Esther Stenson, and Eric Trinka, who read portions or all of the manuscript and offered insightful feedback and useful critique.

Without the friendship and support of Jacob Lester, I would not have persisted in finding a way to publish this book, nor been able to successfully navigate the technical requirements of publication.

ACKNOWLEDGMENTS

I am grateful to Bonnie Bowser, Marci Frederick, and Jennifer Ulrich of EMU's Hartzler Library, who procured many interlibrary loan materials, checked regularly on the progress of the manuscript, provided a hospitable work space, and plied me with coffee.

The persistent cheerleading of Karen King, Linda Pickwell, and Sheryl Shenk sustained me.

Over decades it has been a joy to dive into the treasures of the biblical languages with Andrea Early, Reta Finger, Vasiliki Limberis, Sarah Lind, Anil Solanki, Dorothy Jean Weaver, and Robert Wright.

Always, I bless the memory of my mother and father Velma and Wilmer Heisey, who encouraged, nay insisted, that I get to know the Bible; and also of my husband Paul Longacre, reader extraordinaire of God's book of nature. When I spent too long buried in papers and books, Paul would say, "You need to go out and get some dirt under your fingernails."

Introduction

Recently worship in my Mennonite congregation included an event when the pastors called forward twelve-year-old children and their parents, and presented each young person with a Bible. "These stories are our stories," the pastors told the group gathered before us. As I observed the parents and their children, images of twelve-year-old Jesus in the temple with the elders (Luke 2) flitted through my mind, and then bumped into memories of my nephew's Bar Mitzvah at his synagogue. As in my congregation, so in many communities of faith, pastors, Sunday school teachers, and study group leaders work hard to connect biblical stories with the lives of the people who participate.

Teaching Bible to college undergraduates for over twenty years, though, I learned how few of the Bible stories my students actually knew—whether they had grown up in congregations like mine or had only been in church once or twice, perhaps with grandparents. So, giving people Bibles is only the first step. Finding ways to encourage reading the Bible is the next step, or a series of steps. The pastors in our congregation didn't say that the Bible is God's story, although I am sure they assumed that concept as a foundation for this special event. For some of us present that Sunday, the equation: "the Bible is God's Word" had shaped our earliest experiences of listening to Bible stories and learning to read it for ourselves. But for many readers, paying attention to the Bible has given rise to many questions about how that equation really works. Learning from theological declarations and arguments about the Bible as God's Word is important work, a lifelong task, for people of faith.

As a university instructor, I started out with this basic explanation of the Bible as God's Word: the Bible contains the one great story of God's steadfast love for humanity and for all creation. And that saving love was fully revealed to us in the life, teachings, death, and resurrection of Jesus

INTRODUCTION

Christ. I hoped that such foundation could also be a springboard for the longer and more complex task of learning the Bible's story and applying it to our own world. But I discovered delving into God's love story was not all that was needed. As my students explored biblical accounts, they frequently had questions that surrounded what they were reading.

What follows in this book picks up some of those questions. Each chapter begins with a question, and taken together they trace the journey my students and I have taken over the years, both into the biblical text and into what surrounds it. Readers may want to go straight through all the questions, which are arranged somewhat chronologically. Or you may enter in to one specific question that you have wondered about. As you read, it will soon be obvious that within each question is a series of more related things to ponder. For the Bible as we know it, whatever format we use, also has a story. I hope readers will begin to unpack ways that the Bible's story intersects with our stories. Perhaps the twelve-year-olds who received those Bibles, or their parents, or some of my students, or any Bible readers, find themselves asking: "Wait, what?! Who recorded Moses talking to God? Do we have any artifacts from King Solomon's temple? Why did Prophet Isaiah think King Cyrus of Persia was a messiah? If Jesus never wrote anything, how do we really know what he said and did? Who copied down and distributed Paul's letters? And how did all that ancient writing get into English, or Spanish, or Chinese?"

Such questions are appropriate and important, yet sometimes they worry readers who wonder whether asking them detracts from taking the Bible seriously as God's Word. The story that surrounds the Bible is a very human story, spreading across global history and geography, and involving complex political, economic, and cultural interactions. For some scholars, the humanity of these stories diminishes or even destroys claims of divine activity within Scripture. Yet, I think that learning more about the work of storytellers, scribes, translators, and commentators offers us instead a rich account of human efforts inspired and shaped by God's wisdom and presence. As New Testament scholar Dennis Edwards puts it, "The Bible is the supreme example of divine-human collaboration."[1] That declaration is a faith claim. It insists that God has always been willing to use humans in sharing God's love story.

The first chapter introduces an essential question twenty-first-century readers must consider: What does it mean that we encounter the Bible in

---

1. Edwards, *What Is the Bible?*, 30.

INTRODUCTION

our own languages, and how did it get to words we understand, from the ancient tongues in which it was first heard? Throughout this chapter and the entire book, I offer biblical references that readers can look up if desired. All biblical quotations are from the New Revised Standard Version (NRSV) unless otherwise noted. Chapters 2 through 5 deal with some of the most difficult questions in the Bible's history, because they depend on scholarly theories that may draw on physical evidence but are not always certain. Since the texts of the Bible are not nearly as old as the stories the Bible tells, understanding as much as possible about those theories and the evidence we have requires care and clarity. Chapters 6 through 9 delve into what is known about how biblical texts were copied, edited, selected, and distributed across the world. Finally, we will consider questions about how modern and contemporary readers have described God's Spirit at work shaping human writing and transmitting of God's story.

Each chapter also includes excerpts of texts by people who played a role in bringing the Bible to us. Throughout, I write as a Christian, yet I must underline that much of this story also belongs to Jews, with whom Christians share a large portion of the Bible. While I am an outsider to Jewish faith, I am clear that failing to note our shared heritage seriously limits the story. Readers may also wonder what I believe about the Bible, as is your right. Throughout this book I have tried to present as much accurate information as possible, and to recount it so that people of different backgrounds and views can give this information due consideration. My own journey with the Bible goes back to the days of early childhood when my mother helped me memorize Scripture. Over the years I sometimes backed away from the Bible, finding it confining or even insulting to me and my world. But decades of reading, study, and praying Scripture, both formally and informally, have drawn me back to loving the Bible. I am grateful that both the communities to which I belong and my personal commitments are sustained with this confident message: "The unfolding of your words gives light" (Ps 119:130).

Chapter 1

What Does It Mean to Read the Bible in Translation?

Genesis, the first book in the Bible, includes a story about how human communication was "confused," so that people were no longer able to talk with each other (Gen 11:1–9). The story raises interesting theological questions; for example, why does God mix up the languages, in response to human plans which include "making a name for ourselves," and "not being scattered over the earth"? These questions reveal that early biblical storytellers both experienced and wondered about whether linguistic diversity was part of God's plan. Perhaps they were also considering benefits and drawbacks of reaching across the barriers set up by their differences with the peoples around them.

Of course, Israelite narrators were not the first to think about such matters. Herodotus, a Greek ethno-historian who wrote four centuries before New Testament times, passed along a story from Carthaginians about a silent trade they carried out with other Africans. Each side placed their items for trade, goods or gold, on a river bank and then took turns checking their exchange until each agreed that the trade amount was fair. No matter how historically accurate this report may be, Herodotus described the ancient human desire and need to communicate when they did not share a spoken or written language. Even earlier than Herodotus or the Genesis writers, written texts, whether engraved in stone or inked onto parchment, needed to be translated. Often these documents spelled out political or legal agreements. A treaty or a contract needed to be distributed to all those affected. Rulers expected the territories they had conquered to recognize who was in charge. These ancient written translations reflected the perspective of literate members at the very top of their culture's hierarchies.

A well-known example of such translation is the Rosetta Stone, discovered in Egypt by French military officers in 1799. This stone monument, likely set up in an Egyptian temple compound, was inscribed by Egyptian priests to celebrate the coronation of King Ptolemy V in 196 BCE. The sacred language of the priests was expressed in hieroglyphic, but the language of Ptolemy, a Hellenistic ruler whose dynasty descended from Alexander the Great, was Greek. In the middle section of the stone, the scribes inserted the text in Demotic Egyptian, the script derived from ancient hieroglyphic, and at the bottom provided a translation into Greek. This monument became the foundation of modern work to decipher ancient hieroglyphics.

Modern scholars who study translation practices and theories point out that "translation" as a concept can cover a very broad range of situations, as noted in the story of ancient African non-verbal trading. In modern settings, turning a book into a movie, or a scholarly lecture into a popular article, are both kinds of translation. But in professional terms, "Translators write, interpreters speak." Thus, in this book, when we speak of translation, we are talking about the work of rendering one written language into another.

Since the Bible's texts were written down in ancient Hebrew or Aramaic, and in Koine Greek, people who hear or read the Bible in twenty-first-century languages necessarily encounter Scripture in translation. Whatever the translators' methodology, they have taken on the task of carefully considering the written text in the source language, and seek to shape accurate and clear expressions in a receptor language. We will consider several stories where Bible translation took place, pay attention to how that translation influenced geographic spread of faith communities, and look at some of the knotty problems that translators face.

The story of Bible translation began in Egypt. For Egyptians as well as other Mediterranean peoples, being conquered by the armies of the Greek general Alexander the Great (356–323 BCE) forced them into an encounter with Greek knowledge, culture, and language. Alexander, ruler of Macedonia, had been educated by the Greek philosopher Aristotle. He boasted that he had conquered territory from India to Ethiopia, but Mediterranean peoples felt most strongly the force of their conqueror's commitment to Greek religion, philosophy, and language. In Egypt, both the Rosetta Stone

WHAT DOES IT MEAN TO READ THE BIBLE IN TRANSLATION?

and the Greek translation of the Hebrew Torah, known as the Septuagint, provide evidence of this widespread hellenization.

Egyptian Jews who translated their Scriptures from Hebrew into Greek, however, cared about more than political accommodation. Ancient victory monuments or treaties of conquest of course also had religious underpinnings, yet the Jews had for the most part suffered on the underside of ancient empires. Jews, who were named after the region known by hellenized rulers as Judea, had for centuries been scattered from Babylon to Asia Minor and Egypt, after their own kingdoms were destroyed. Although their stories included much information about their own kings, these stories also reflected perspectives critical of monarchy. Looking back on the captivity and dispersion they had suffered, Jews interpreted what had happened in terms of their failure to keep their ancient covenant with their God YHWH.[1] By the second century BCE, however, many Jews, especially those living in hellenized Egypt, were no longer able to understand their scriptures in Hebrew. A fascinating text from the second century BCE described how the Torah, that is, the first five books of the Bible, were translated from Hebrew into Greek.

> 1.1 The Letter of Aristeas, *ostensibly from an Alexandrian Jew to his brother, detailed how King Ptolemy of Egypt urged the librarian of Alexandria to acquire all the world's books, translated into Greek. The high priest in Jerusalem was requested to send seventy-two scholars, six for each of the twelve tribes, to Egypt to translate the Torah. In this section, the letter writer explained the translators' daily practice as they worked.*
>
> At the first hour of the day [the Torah scholars from Jerusalem] attended the court daily, and after saluting [King Ptolemy] retired to their own quarters. Following the custom of all the Jews, they washed their hands in the sea in the course of their prayers to God, and then proceeded to the reading and explication of each point. . . . They explained that [washing hands] is evidence that they have done no evil, for all activity takes place by means of the hands. Thus they nobly and piously refer everything to righteousness and truth. In this way, as we said previously, each day they assembled in their quarters, which were pleasantly situated for quiet and light, and proceeded to fulfill their prescribed task. The

---

1. This book uses the Hebrew four-letter name of God YHWH when describing or quoting the Hebrew biblical text. It appears as LORD in many modern English translations. The author also uses "Divine Name" when describing Jewish practices regarding God's name.

outcome was such that in seventy-two days, the business of translation was completed, just as if such a result was achieved by some deliberate design.[2]

Scholars agree that the *Letter* is fictional, but also that the story represented an important cultural moment in the ancient world. First, it described different cultural and religious traditions, and how faithful Jews and learned pagans met each other with mutual respect. By the time the *Letter* was written, although the text recounted the desire of Hellenistic rulers to have access to the Torah, it is likely that hellenized Jews were the primary audience for the translation. It also underlined that Jews possessed sacred writings that were important to them, and wanted those texts to be widely accessible.[3] Of equal importance was this text's claim of a divine role in the translation. The translation that developed during this period came to be known as the Septuagint (LXX). This Roman-numeral acronym shorthand refers to the seventy-two (in some accounts seventy) translators reported in the *Letter*. Many Jesus-believers used primarily the LXX, as they told the stories of Jesus and explained how those stories were based on their Bible. The Bible in Greek was also the primary text for gentiles who became part of the Jesus community.

Some centuries after the first Greek translations, Jews living in Babylon began translating and commenting on the Torah in Aramaic, a sister language to Hebrew, in forms called targumim, or "interpretations." Although many rabbis continued to read and interpret the texts in Hebrew, the targumim remained useful in some Jewish communities. The targumim are also consulted regularly by modern textual scholars, because they offer both a different window on translation, and some of the interpretational methods emerging in Jewish communities.

Early Christians carried forward the Jewish heritage of translating the Bible. By the third century CE, portions of writings that became known as the New Testament had been translated into Syriac, from the same linguistic family as Hebrew; Coptic, the descendent of Demotic Egyptian, and Old Latin, primarily in North Africa.

---

2. *Letter of Aristeas*, vv. 303–7.
3. Carter, *Seven Events*, 21–42.

WHAT DOES IT MEAN TO READ THE BIBLE IN TRANSLATION?

As the Christian movement spread, Bible portions also traveled far beyond the Mediterranean world. Merchants had been traveling eastward along the ancient Silk Road, which ended in the west in Antioch, since the second century BCE. In the seventh century CE, Christian monks traveling with the merchants received entrée to the capital of the Chinese Tang Dynasty. A Syriac-speaking Persian monk, Alopen, was authorized by the imperial court to translate the texts brought with him, including parts of the Bible. Several manuscripts discovered in nearby caves, dating from the time of Alopen, offered fascinating glimpses of the translation practices of the Persian monks. For example, the monks adopted Chinese terms such as "Cool Wind" for the Holy Spirit. But elsewhere they transliterated Syriac words, specifically using *Ye-su* for "Jesus." A monument set up in 781 CE in Shaanxi Province to mark this Christian presence included an overview of the biblical story: "Therefore my Lord Ye Su, the One emanating in three subtle bodies, hid his true power, became a human, and came on behalf of the Lord of Heaven to preach the good tidings."[4] While imperial favor of the Tang rulers was later withdrawn from the Christians, and no lasting Christian community was established in China at that time, this monument had kept a record of one early effort at Bible translation.

In early centuries, Bible translations were recognized primarily for their usefulness. However, the fear that translators were in some way misrepresenting, or even corrupting, the text, was soon expressed.

> 1.2 *Jerome, a fourth-century CE Roman scholar and monk, faced such criticism. Best known for his influential translation known as the Latin Vulgate, Jerome's efforts were not always applauded. In Letter 57, to his advisor the Roman senator Pammachius, Jerome defended himself against charges of his opponents.*
>
> For I myself not only admit but freely proclaim that in translating from the Greek (except in the case of the holy scriptures where even the order of the words is a mystery) I render sense for sense and not word for word.... That secular and church writers should have adopted this line need not surprise us when we consider that the translators of the Septuagint, the evangelists, and the apostles, have done the same in dealing with the sacred writings. We read in Mark of the Lord saying Talitha cumi and it is immediately added "which is interpreted, Damsel, I say unto thee, arise." The evangelist may be charged with falsehood for having added the words "I say unto thee" for the Hebrew is only "Damsel arise." To emphasize

---

4. Coakley and Sterk, "Xian Inscription," 244.

this and to give the impression of one calling and commanding he has added "I say unto thee." . . .

I have exceeded the limits of a letter, but I have not exceeded in the expression of my chagrin. For, though I am called a falsifier, and have my reputation torn to shreds, wherever there are shuttles and looms and women to work them; I am content to repudiate the charge without retaliating in kind. . . . For the rest, I am satisfied to have instructed one of my dearest friends and am content simply to stay quiet in my cell and to wait for the day of judgment.[5]

Bible translation in Europe also became more controversial during the Middle Ages. Jerome's Latin translation became known as the Vulgate. Originally expressed in everyday Latin (hence the name Vulgate, meaning common), this version came to prominence as the Bible in western Europe. In the ninth century, Greek-speaking missionaries from Constantinople, Cyril and Methodius, encountered the political and religious opposition of Latin-speaking authorities when they arrived in Moravia. Tensions had been simmering between western Christians under the authority of the church in Rome and eastern churches under Constantinople. Among their differences were the languages of the Bible. Eastern churches used the Greek Bible but were accustomed to translating it into other languages. In the West, the Latin Vulgate was widely understood by religious leaders as the most "sacred" language.

Rulers in Constantinople had sent Cyril and Methodius as missionaries to Moravia in response to a request from a local prince. This request likely was political as well as religious, because nobles in central Europe were constantly negotiating alliances with either eastern or western emperors. Because the Slavic people of the region had no alphabet for their language, Cyril and Methodius started by developing a script to write in Slavic, called Glagolitic. Cyril then began to translate Bible portions as well as liturgical materials. German-speaking princes and church leaders in the region, whose allegiance was to the church in Rome, pushed back. They claimed that there were only three "holy languages": Hebrew, Greek, and Latin. Eventually the brothers traveled to Rome to seek papal approval for their work. They did receive official affirmation, and were allowed to celebrate the Mass in Slavonic while there. However, after commissioning his

---

5. Jerome, *Letter* 57.5, 7, 13.

brother to continue the work in Moravia, Cyril died in Rome. Methodius returned to Moravia to continue his mission. The conflict was not entirely resolved, for Methodius was again arrested and imprisoned for a time in a German monastery.[6]

Elsewhere over the centuries, European colonial empires rose, moving their armies and commercial interests across the world. Christian missionaries almost always followed. As the story of Cyril and Methodius illustrated, making the Bible available to new regions often first required creating an alphabet so that the language could be written. While critics point out that the intersection of European colonialism and missionary efforts at times corrupted the Christian message, others note the importance to many local cultures of missionary efforts to help people write and read in their own languages. One early modern missionary story shows this complex interaction.

The Indian subcontinent, like China, had an ancient literary tradition. Christians had been part of life in South India from the fifth century CE, using the Syriac-language Bible brought there with Christians from Persia. English colonial and trading forces established their presence in northern India in the eighteenth century. Toward the end of that century, William Carey, an English Baptist, felt called to go to India as a missionary. Carey recognized that he needed to learn Indian languages and understand something of Indian culture. In 1792 he wrote: "As to learning their languages . . . the missionaries must have patience, and mingle with the people, till they have learned so much of their language as to be able to communicate their ideas to them in it."[7] Despite his claim about the necessity of learning the language of the people he contacted, Carey began his study with India's ancient literary language, Sanskrit. He also developed a written grammar for the study of Sanskrit, eventually translating much of the epic *The Ramayana* into English.

Carey, however, was not trained in linguistics. He learned the languages from written texts, and was not familiar with idioms or everyday usage. He was not prepared to make good used of the expertise of his Indian assistants. Using a word-for-word method, his translations ended up sounding wooden or incomprehensible to Indians. As a Baptist, Carey also had a political problem. To the English colonial authorities, who were Anglican, he was seen as a dissenter. Thus, the colonial political authorities

---

6. Fletcher, *Conversion of Europe*, 351–56.
7. Carey, *Enquiry into the Obligations of Christians*, 3–4.

often ignored or obstructed his work. Still, Carey's remarkable work has continued through Serampore College, founded in 1800. Serampore is still actively training Indian leaders today. But none of Carey's biblical translations were ever widely used in Indian Christian communities.

In the twentieth century Gambian theologian Lamin Sanneh wrote an extensive history of Bible translation efforts by Christian missionaries around the world. He offered examples of translators clashing with colonial authorities for preaching and teaching in local languages and noted where missionaries had developed grammars of local languages. Sanneh declared: "The seeds of the divergence between mission and colonialism were sown with the translation enterprise."[8] While Sanneh acknowledged as well that missionary efforts sometimes harmed cultures where they went, he argued that promoting literacy in local languages helped many peoples build needed skills to resist colonial authority.

One example of the process Sanneh described is in the work of Bishop Samuel Ajayi Crowther, appointed in 1864 to lead the Anglican church in the Niger Delta of West Africa. Crowther, a renowned linguist, translated the Bible, developed a dictionary, and published a Yoruba language grammar. African clergy who worked with him translated the Bible and liturgical materials into several other languages of the region.[9]

According to the United Bible Societies, over seven hundred languages now have complete translations of the Bible. In the twenty-first century translators around the globe are well trained, from many language backgrounds, with electronic access to textual materials and linguistic consultants. Good editions of the Hebrew and Greek texts from which translators work are widely accessible. Yet the task of translation is continuous, since modern languages change, new biblical commentaries become available, and research in the ancient documents sometimes unearths new details about the context of the ancient writing. Much literature on translation theory and approaches to specific translation dilemmas has been written. In the following section we will consider just a few such matters.

What if the original text can be read in more than one way?

Ancient Hebrew and Greek words describing the character of God, or expressing desired behavior by God's people, often come with rich ranges

8. Sanneh, *Translating the Message*, 111.
9. Brockman, "Crowther, Samuel Ajayi."

of meaning both in the source languages and in a variety of receptor languages. One such term is the Greek word *dikaiosune*. (Hebrew has several words that were translated into Greek as *dikaiosune*.) In English language versions, this word has traditionally been translated as "righteousness." In languages such as Spanish and French, the word is usually translated as "justice." To English speakers, these two terms may sound quite different; the connotation of "righteousness" is more spiritual, while "justice" sounds more like a legal term. This difference is lodged in the history of the development of the English language. "Righteousness" is a word coming from Old English, while "justice" entered English through the Anglo-Norman/French language. For contemporary English translators, however, using "justice" in English is a very accurate rendering. Biblical readers must be invited to ponder what the apostle Paul meant when he said, "The *dikaiosune* of God is revealed through faith for faith" (Rom 1:17). What new understandings arise when "justice" is read, rather than "righteousness"?

What if there is no one-to-one equivalent in the receiving language?

Students learning a second language usually enjoy making the connection from one language to another. "Cat" is *gato* in Spanish, or *mósí* in Navajo. Sometimes, however, words that appear to move directly across languages can also confuse. "Librairie" in French is not "library" in English; it means "bookstore." And contemporary Bible translators must work around places where there is no specific equivalent word in the receptor languages. For example, bears do not live in Africa. To render the story when David described to Saul killing a lion and a bear (1 Sam 17:34), African translators often use a descriptor such as "'wild,' 'ferocious' or 'dangerous animal.'"[10]

Equally complicated are places where the receptor language has multiple words for one Hebrew or Greek word. During the translation of the Navajo Bible, in the 1950s, Faye Edgerton and Navajo colleagues dealt with the complexity of Navajo family language. In Greek, and in English, there is one word for "sister." In Navajo, however, siblings are labeled according to whether they are older or younger. In Luke's story of Martha and Mary, the translation team had to determine which sister was older. After discussion,

---

10. Zogbo, "Issues in Bible Translation," 281.

they concluded that Martha was "older sister" because she demanded that Mary should help her.[11]

Should translators focus more on the source/original or on the receiving language?

This is one of the biggest questions in biblical translations. As noted above, translations like Carey's focused on a word-for-word approach, which can produce texts that are hard to read or even nonsensical. Martin Luther, who prepared one of the earliest German Bible translations, insisted on finding words and expressions that sounded like sixteenth-century German speech. But Luther also made choices that were more theological than cultural. For example, he "used one German verb, '*predigen* = preach,' for the translation of more than thirty [New Testament] Greek verbs having to do with verbal communication."[12]

In the twentieth century, Eugene Nida, a world-renowned translator and theoretician, argued for focus to be on meaning in receptor languages. Nida articulated the concept of "dynamic equivalence," which asserted that meaning is found in phrases or even combinations of sentences, rather than in single words. Translations should thus seek to express the cultural givens of receptor languages. When asked about his most important contribution to Bible translation, Nida replied: "To help people be willing to say what the text means—not what the words are, but what the text means."[13]

How do individual and committee translations differ?

Throughout the history of Bible translation, many translations have been carried out by one person, even if that person was assisted by scribes or students. Jerome is famous for the first widely used Latin version, Martin Luther did the translation into German that shaped centuries of German language usage, and William Tyndale prepared the first major New Testament translation into modern English. Today most widely used versions are instead carried out by many scholars, under the direction of editorial committees. The Common English Bible, a version first published in 2011,

---

11. Wallis, *God Speaks Navajo*, 103–4.
12. Guder, *Called to Witness*, 89.
13. Neff, "Meaning-Full Translations," 46.

lists an editorial board of ten members, and names more than one hundred translators with their academic affiliations. Yet particular scholars still undertake their own versions, as do scholarly translators of many other ancient texts. Contemporary readers have been drawn to the work of Eugene Peterson, whose *The Message* was a paraphrase rather than a direct translation; yet Peterson was a well-trained biblical scholar deeply skilled in the original languages. Recent individual translations of all or parts of the New Testament have been completed by Sarah Ruden, a classics scholar and a Quaker; David Bentley Hart, an Eastern Orthodox philosopher and theologian; and Scot McKnight, an Anglican-Anabaptist professor.

Both individual and committee translations can offer insights; the former reflect the gifts and perspectives of their translators, and readers should take note of what their translators are interested in. The latter translations are shaped by broad scholarly consensus, include translators from a spectrum of theological views, and are tested with ordinary readers before publication.

What should translators do with controversial words and phrases?

In the twentieth century, translators and readers argued about whether and how much to make the biblical text more inclusive, as contemporary cultures focused more on class and gender identities. One frequent decision has been to translate the word "brothers," especially when the apostle Paul addressed his churches with that term, as "brothers and sisters." Some readers add "and siblings," for even greater inclusion. Most translations who use this approach provide a footnote indicating what the word was in the original language.

Another problem is the translation of New Testament texts that use the Greek word *Ioudaioi*. Christian theologians after the Holocaust in Europe were forced to admit that biblical interpretation contributed to the genocidal policies of the Third Reich. In its earliest uses, *Ioudaioi* identified people from the territory of Judea. Yet the term was also quickly associated with the faith and practices of both Judean and diaspora Jewish communities. The 1975 New King James reads: "But the Jews did not believe concerning him, that he had been blind and received his sight." Recent translations have chosen to render the Greek term more narrowly. So, the 2011 Common English Bible translates: "The Jewish leaders didn't believe the man had been blind and received his sight" (John 9:18). Translators face issues related to Jewish beliefs and practices throughout the Bible, and ways to assure respectful and accurate wording are often contested.

How should words with significant theological content be translated?

The earliest biblical manuscripts already show that scribes granted special importance to words about God. In some ancient Hebrew manuscripts written in square Aramaic characters, the four-letter divine name YHWH, the tetragrammaton, continued to be copied in old Hebrew script. Later, in early Christian texts, words such as "Jesus" and "savior" were copied with abbreviations, using the first and last letters of the word (IS for *Iesous*). In modern translations, Western-trained scholars often have avoided using local words for God, the Holy Spirit, and other "sacred" terms, concerned that they might improperly or inadequately convey the correct theological meaning. Recently, however, translation consultants have argued that words for spiritual beings and concepts, as used in receptor languages, will best help readers to understand biblical theological perspectives.

For example, the first Kipende New Testament translation in the Democratic Republic of Congo used a Greek loan-word, *nyuma* (*pneuma*) for "spirit," together with the Pende adjective for "good" to refer to the Holy Spirit. In the 1970s, however, translators decided instead to use the word *givuli* (closer to the idea of "wind"). Likewise, translations into indigenous languages in Latin America for many years used "Diyo," or another form taken from the Spanish *Dios*, rather than a name or word particular to the indigenous language.[14]

How can translators move beyond re-colonizing Bible translations?

As already noted, missionaries have for centuries played important roles in Bible translations. Despite the many benefits of that commitment to making the Bible available in diverse languages, contemporary translators must recognize that aspects of this task have been shaped by outside organizations, rather than the needs and interests of those who will receive their

---

14. Sánchez-Cetina, "Word of God," 394.

work. For example, for many years some translators used major language versions, rather than Hebrew and Greek, to translate into languages of small groups. English, Spanish and French Bible versions have served as the primary sources for versions in Ndebele, Kekchi, or Kikongo. Academically trained translators can also fail to take into account that recipients of current translations may be more oriented to listening or seeing than reading. And lack of care for class and gender realities often shapes choices. Sánchez-Cetina notes the tradition in Spanish versions of calling Naaman's servant (2 Kgs 5) a "young woman." Instead, he argues, the Hebrew indicates a child. It matters, he asserts, that, "A simple 'girl' and not a 'young woman' who also happened to be a war victim was the instrument of healing and liberation for Naaman, the person who was the cause of her bondage."[15]

So, the entire history of the Bible is a history of translation. Woven through this story are both failures and successes. Translators have encountered many-faceted challenges, some that were acknowledged centuries ago, and others that arise as new linguistic, political, and social realities emerge around the world. Yet the desire to hear God speak through Scripture remains strong, and human decisions to act faithfully in response to that Word keep showing up around the world. The story of Bible translation helps readers and hearers better understand how humans have been actors in the journey of the Bible from when it was first spoken into the present. For faith communities, the stories of translation reveal evidence of the action of God's Spirit throughout the process. Learning about translation also pushes us to look into other questions about this story, beginning with how the earliest accounts of God's work and word were recorded.

---

15. Sánchez-Cetina, "Word of God," 400.

Chapter 2

How Did Ancient Stories Become Hebrew Scrolls?

After considering what it means to read the Bible in modern languages, we turn to what is known about the languages of the earliest biblical stories. While some Bible readers may long to see the original Hebrew manuscripts that lie behind the work of translators, no such manuscripts exist. Apart from two small silver scrolls, etched in ancient Hebrew letters and dated to the late seventh or early sixth-century BCE, the earliest manuscripts used to study and translate the Bible from both Hebrew and Greek come from shortly before the time when Jesus lived.

The Bible itself, however, is little concerned with how it came to be written, focusing rather on the powerful spoken word of God. The Bible shared by Christians and Jews opens with a dramatic claim, "In the beginning God created" (Gen 1:1). This creation took place as God spoke.[1] When the Israelites received the Law at Mount Sinai, their promise reflected this same spoken character: "All the words that the LORD *has spoken* we will do" (Exod 24:3). In language that continued among the biblical prophets, Samuel told Saul, the first king of Israel, "Now therefore *listen to the word* of the LORD" (1 Sam 15:1). And the psalmist repeated the creation account: "*By the word* of the LORD the heavens were made" (Ps 33:6).[2]

---

1. An opening Jewish morning prayer underlines the creative power of God's word: "Blessed is the One who spoke all things into being."

2. The italics in this paragraph are the emphasis of the author.

HOW DID ANCIENT STORIES BECOME HEBREW SCROLLS?

The biblical assertion that the God who speaks is the main character is at the heart of Scripture. While readers over the centuries have proposed varied ways of interpreting the Bible, no human being has ever claimed to have heard God's first creating words. The first five books of the Bible, called the Torah or the Pentateuch, recount God's actions in a way that has nothing to do with manuscripts: first at the creation of the cosmos, and then among ancestors who journeyed at God's command. Scripture storytellers shared their experiences, memories, and visions of God, and many of those stories described hearing God speak. For example, God called to Hagar in the desert (Gen 21), to Moses at the burning bush (Exod 3), to the boy Samuel (1 Sam 3), and with "a sound of sheer silence" to the prophet Elijah at Mount Horeb (1 Kgs 19). These storytellers experienced God as "merciful and gracious, slow to anger, and abounding in steadfast love and faithfulness" (Exod 34:6). Readers and hearers ever since have understood, in some way, that those stories, in human language, are the words of this God.

Thus, contemporary readers who are used to imagining a traceable thread from the writing of ancient authors to the copying and publishing of those words face a challenge. We must look back from the earliest written materials, through centuries of history, some of it accounted for in other records, and some of it referenced in the Bible itself. The next three chapters will explain what can be known or suggested about the process that led to writing down of the biblical texts now studied by modern scholars. First, we will discuss the relationship between oral and written accounts, and consider what led to the first formal writing in Israel. In chapter 4 we will discuss a key historical reference point, the Babylonian destruction of Jerusalem (597–587 BCE), and how this crisis motivated the collection and editing of Israel's story. Chapter 5 explores the impact of the Greek and then Roman conquests of the Mediterranean, not long before the life of Jesus, and how this colonization shaped Scripture in written form for those who wanted to obey God's commands to God's people.[3]

How, then, did ancient people move from recounting their earliest understandings of God to producing scrolls, and eventually book-form codices? In the twenty-first century, most people hold one of the following mental images of this process: some imagine God's word, beginning with the creation story, dropping out of heaven written on tablets. Others picture

---

3. The content of chapters 3 and 4 is indebted to the work of David M. Carr, especially *Formation of the Hebrew Bible* (2011). Any mistakes or misrepresentations of Carr's work are the author's responsibility. A briefer outline of the history of Israel related to the biblical text can be found in Steven L. McKenzie, "Israel, History of," in *NIDB* 3:117–31.

human scribes carefully writing down the stories and explanations as God dictated to them. Still other contemporary readers, who agree that ancient storytellers were speaking for God, declare that those tellers recorded what happened using their own languages and cultural, geographical, and political settings. Yet others assert that everything in the Bible is a work of human imagination, and thus the Bible is a human document rather than a divine message.

The Bible does not set out to prove any of those views.[4] Beginning with the Torah, it makes three claims. First, Scripture asserts that God is creator of everything, and as creator is also God of all people. Second, God called a particular people into a special relationship, a covenant, so that they could be a sign and an invitation to the world. Third, God liberated this people from enslavement with the command to worship only God and to live justly with their neighbors. The texts through which these themes are developed recounted how God's people responded, spelled out detailed laws to govern the practices that should shape God's people, and offered people's prayers and questions back to God.

All parts of the Bible are set in places on the world's maps. The Bible as a human artifact originated in Mesopotamia, Egypt, and in the narrow land bridge between these two ancient superpowers. Genesis recounts that Abraham and Sarah, Israel's first ancestors, heard God's call to leave their home in Mesopotamia (now Iraq) and to travel to Canaan. Exodus opens with the story of Moses, a descendent of Abraham and Sarah, who was born into slavery in Egypt, adopted into the household of Egypt's ruler, and emerged to lead the Israelites out of Egypt. Both Abraham and Moses are central characters in the Torah, whose stories and memories loom large in New Testament conversations. Since neither Abraham and Sarah nor Moses appear in historical records, a helpful way to read their stories is to understand the forms, or genres, in which these towering biblical figures are portrayed.

A long and important section of text in the Torah is the narrative that can be described by the literary term *saga*. This term came into English from its use in Scandinavian languages, where it referred to oral structured narratives about their heroes. While sagas are not based on historical documents, and took shape as they were orally transmitted, they are understood

---

4. Chapters 3 and 4 use the term "Bible" to refer to the collection of writings known as the Old Testament by Christians. This collection is the Bible/Tanakh read by Jews today, as well as the Scripture studied and quoted by Jesus and his first followers.

as factual and meaningful in their cultures. Many cultures have told stories about their ancient past in similar ways. The Babylonian *Epic of Gilgamesh*, the Old English *Beowulf*, or the medieval account of Emperor Sundiata of Mali provide analogies. Within the saga of Abraham and Sarah, and their descendants, the Torah also includes many smaller segments, or sub-genres. For example, there are theophanies (Moses's meeting God at the burning bush, in Exod 3); etiologies (explanations of the origin of something, as in Isaac's name, "laughter," in Gen 21); hymns (Miriam's song when the Israelites crossed the Red Sea, in Exod 15), and genealogies (lists of ancestors, as in Gen 5).

In addition to narrative, the Torah also contains many laws, beginning with the foundational Ten Words, or Ten Commandments, given by God to Moses (Exod 20). In Hebrew, the first definition of the word *torah* is "law." Lodged within the Torah's broad narrative, the laws spelled out how to keep Israel's covenant with God, and what actions were required to live in right relationships with each other and their neighbors. The Ten Words and the rest of the laws that expanded on them were given to Moses by God at Mount Sinai. At first God self-identified as the God of Moses's ancestors, but when Moses pressed for the Divine Name, God revealed to Moses the name YHWH, used frequently throughout the rest of the Old Testament.

Moses's role within the story was significant first because he was the link back to the patriarchs and matriarchs of the saga. But Moses also moved the story forward, as he led the people out of enslavement in Egypt, and as he received the revelation of God's Law. Ancient tradition named Moses as author of the whole Torah, as both Jesus and Paul declared (Luke 24; 2 Cor 3). In the Torah's final work, Deuteronomy, Moses was portrayed as he reviewed Israel's ancient story and repeated the law. Yet Deuteronomy also described problems faced by God's people after their time wandering in the wilderness, when they would be under kingly rule. It also detailed a new understanding of God's covenant with Israel, a covenant of divine blessing for obedience, but the promise of curses if the people disobeyed. The historical narratives that follow the Torah underlined this Deuteronomistic theology, and the proclamations of Israel's prophets reiterated these claims. According to Deuteronomy, Moses told the people that later God would send them "a prophet like me," underlining the towering Mosaic influence over the writings beyond the Torah (Deut 18:15).

Yet even early readers recognized that Moses could not have been the author of everything in the Torah. Medieval rabbinic commentator Ibn

Ezra (ca. 1089–1167), in his massive commentary on the Torah, underlined that the text of Deuteronomy clarified the limit of Mosaic authorship. "In my opinion, [Deut 34] was written by Joshua. Once Moses went up the mountain, he certainly did not write any more."[5]

Much modern Torah scholarship has assumed that ancient biblical accounts, such as the saga of Abraham's and Sarah's descendants, or the laws revealed to Moses, were first transmitted orally. According to one scholar: "To comprehend the written Bible, it is essential to understand that most of the words which are now written down in it had been spoken first and had been heard long before they could ever have been read."[6] Torah texts also point in that direction, directing that elders in later generations should be prepared for particular questions: "And when your children ask, 'What do you mean by this observance?' you shall say, 'It is the passover sacrifice to YHWH'" (Exod 12:26–27). Describing the period later when biblical texts were being copied, another scholar has proposed that scribes collected "pieces of Moses tradition and work[ed] them together."[7]

Traditionally, the theory of oral transmission of ancient stories has been accompanied by the belief that oral communication was more primitive than written texts. Yet mid-twentieth-century studies of story-telling poets in Yugoslavia, observing how these singers performed ancient stories without scripts, proposed a different understanding. Rather than assuming that these singers were reciting word-for-word, observers recognized that the poets were shaping their accounts for their audiences. They were not simply repeating what they had memorized, but taking into account their immediate settings, drawing both faithfully and creatively on their traditions.

Biblical scholars have found this concept of oral performance helpful. Oral patterns use different forms from writing, as attentive speakers and readers recognize, and as linguists and sociologists explain. Spoken discourse repeats words and uses vocalized pauses, while writing reflects more careful word choice. Speakers use intonation, stress, and tone of voice to reflect meaning, while writers use punctuation and description to cover the same information. Grammatical forms of speech are simpler, and often circle back to the same information, while written style introduces new

---

5 Carasik, *Commentators Bible*, 256.
6. Pelikan, *Whose Bible Is It?*, 9.
7. Barton, *History of the Bible*, 55.

HOW DID ANCIENT STORIES BECOME HEBREW SCROLLS?

information at a faster pace, and uses a greater variety of vocabulary, more abstract terms and more complicated grammatical patterns.[8]

For centuries people trying to identify the origins of biblical scrolls, "worked with assumptions of print-like sources and publisher-like redactor-editors," according to Carr.[9] These assumptions evolved in Torah studies into what is known as the Documentary Hypothesis, which identified and labeled sections within the Torah by characteristics of supposed authors and other literary features.

> 2.2 *This Bible dictionary excerpt explains the theory that the biblical texts, especially in the Torah, were put together using earlier written sources. Scholars named these theoretical sources using the acronym JEPD. They based their analysis of these sources on different names or terms used for God as well as other literary or theological markers.*
>
> [The source theory] addressing the formation of the Pentateuch has pride of place. The Documentary Hypothesis involves the claim that the first five books of the OT represent the combination of four distinct sources or "documents." In its classic form, these sources were known as "J," the Yahwistic source ("J" for the German spelling of Yahweh)—e.g., Gen 2:4 b–3:24; "E," the Elohistic source—e.g., Gen 20; "D," the Deuteronomic source—the book of Deuteronomy; and "P," the Priestly source—e.g., Gen 1:1–2:4a. . . . Though many scholars continue to defend this hypothesis, others have offered alternatives, e.g., that the Pentateuch grew from an early narrative with a series of supplements or that, like Samuel, the Pentateuch is made up originally of a series of collections that were combined during the Persian period. Regardless of the fate of the Documentary Hypothesis, few scholars would deny that the creators of the OT used sources. As a result, some form of "source criticism" will remain important in biblical studies.[10]

The 1948 discovery of the Dead Scrolls revealed much older biblical manuscripts than the medieval scrolls which had been used in Torah study and translation. (See chapter 5 for more details on the Dead Sea Scrolls.) These ancient scrolls manifested both significant continuity and curious diversity within the copies. A whole new field of textual scholarship evolved as the

---

8. Bartsch, "Oral Style, Written Style," 41–48.
9. Carr, "Rethinking the Materiality," 595.
10. David L. Petersen, "Source Criticism," in *NIDB* 5:359–60.

Dead Sea Scrolls were published, requiring more nuanced theories about the interrelationship of oral and written stories. Carr refers to "the Israelite scribe as performer, [visible in] several variants found in the parallel Isaiah-Hezekiah narratives and in the ancient [Isaiah] scroll from Qumran."[11] Further, according to Ulrich: "Each [biblical] book is the product not of a single author . . . but of multiple, anonymous bards, sages, religious leaders, compilers, or tradents [those who handed down oral tradition]. Unlike much classical and modern literature, produced by a single, named individual at a single point in time, the biblical books are constituted by earlier traditions being repeated, augmented, and reshaped by later authors, editors, or tradents, over the course of many centuries."[12]

The impact of the Qumran biblical manuscripts on knowledge of the Bible's written forms has been enormous. These ancient scrolls can encourage readers to re-engage the Bible's own claims about God's word. For example, one of the most treasured texts at Qumran repeated the prophetic proclamation from a Judahite in Babylonian exile: "Then the glory of the LORD shall be revealed, and all people shall see it together, for the mouth of the LORD has spoken" (Isa 40:5).

Developing a fuller understanding of how oral and written accounts interact allows contemporary Bible readers to also reconsider data related to the Israelite story from archaeological, geographical, and historical records. Although archeological data do not confirm biblical accounts of the Israelite invasion of Canaan, they do show the development of new cultural patterns in the highlands near the Jordan River in the early Iron Age, when the word "Israel" first appears in the Egyptian Merneptah Stela (see chapter 3). Most biblical accounts take place in a strip of land on the eastern coast of the Mediterranean Sea, about one hundred miles wide and five hundred miles long. Running north and south, four topographic regions shape this region. (On modern maps, this region includes Israel, occupied Palestine, and Jordan.) Its most prominent feature is the Jordan River, part of a geological rift that runs south into Africa. To the east of the river are the Transjordanian mountains, and west of the river are the Palestinian highlands. At the westernmost edge of the land lies the Mediterranean coastal plain.

Written records describe Egyptian control over Palestine in the thirteenth century BCE. As iron technology developed in the twelfth century, city states on Palestine's coastal plain used this advanced metal to

---

11. Carr, "Orality, Textuality and Memory," 163.
12. Ulrich, *Dead Sea Scrolls*, 2.

strengthen their weaponry. Sea-faring Phoenician peoples, known in biblical accounts as Philistines, moved into the area from further north on the Mediterranean coast. These settlers challenged Egyptian control of the territory and brought with them an alphabet used in the first known Israelite inscriptions.

Within this socio-political context, the emergence of Iron Age culture, as seen in archaeological finds, is evident in the highlands that the Bible describes as Israel's first home. One scholar explains: "This evidence came in the form of a host of small villages, mostly unwalled and many newly founded in the early Iron Age, discovered predominantly in the central highlands but also in the Galilee and Negev."[13]

Within these highland settlements, over time, a hierarchical political structure emerged. In the Bible, the Jewish Tanakh, the historical books from Joshua through 2 Kings describe this evolution. Various forms of monarchy had been active for millennia in the world where Israel emerged. These systems were also literate, as evidenced in Sumerian clay tablets and Egyptian hieroglyphic monumental inscriptions. Scholars assume that elite groups of priests and scribes were trained to write and interpret these texts, including accounts of military triumphs, tax and census records, poetry and prayers, and historically oriented sagas.

The biblical histories underline the importance of writing in the Israelite monarchies. Before Israel's first king, Saul, was appointed, the prophet Samuel warned about what kings needed: taxes, military conscription, and slaves (1 Sam 8). The descriptions of both Kings David and Solomon included the names of their "recorders" and "secretaries" (2 Sam 8:16–17; 1 Kgs 4:3). These texts also made forty references to "annals of the king," in their summaries of the reigns of successive rulers, further emphasizing that writing and monarchy went together. Near the end of the kingdom of Judah, the book of Jeremiah describes a dramatic event when King Jehoiakim cut up and burned a scroll on which the prophet had dictated God's condemnation of the king. Jeremiah then ordered his scribe Baruch to rewrite the entire message and return it to the king (Jer 36). Thus, ancient writers emphasized that written texts could be used not only by rulers but in confrontation with them.[14]

Scholars agree that the biblical histories, and most of the prophetic writings, reflect perspectives of the southern kingdom, Judah, where the

---

13. Steven L. McKenzie, "Israel, History of," in *NIDB* 3:117–31.
14. Leuchter, "Jehoiakim and the Scribes," 320–25.

Davidic dynasty held sway for four centuries. "The Bible is a Judean corpus," since the compiling and editing of many of these texts took place among exiled scribes in Babylon after the fall of Jerusalem.[15] External records, however, reveal that Israel, the northern kingdom, played a more prominent role in the region during the earlier ninth and eighth centuries. The Mesha stela (see chapter 3) described the conflict between the Israelite House of Omri and the king of Moab. When the Assyrian Empire finally destroyed Israel's capital in 722 BCE, its ruler boasted of destroying Samaria and taking thousands of Israelites into captivity.

> 2.4 *Sargon II ruled Assyria from 722–705 BCE. This declaration about his brutal victory over Samaria (Samerina) is found in a cuneiform inscription that is part of the Nimrod Prism, dated to 722. This account cross-references the account in 2 Kgs 17, although the biblical description gives the name Shalmaneser to the ruler of Assyria.*
>
> [The inhabitants of Sa]merina, who agreed [and plotted] with a king
> [hostile to] me,
> not to endure servitude and not to bring tribute to Assur and who did battle,
> I fought against them with the power of the great gods, my lords.
> I counted as spoil 27,280 people, together with their chariots, and gods, in
> which they trusted.
> I formed a unit with 200 of [their] chariots for my royal force.
> I settled the rest of them in the midst of Assyria.
> I repopulated Samerina more than before.
> I brought into it people from countries conquered by my hands.
> I appointed my commissioner as governor over them.
> And I counted them as Assyrians.[16]

However the Israelite monarchy evolved, its use of literate information provides more perspective on the earliest biblical writings, according to Carr. While it is likely that the Torah and much of the rest of the Hebrew Scriptures took written form after the destruction of the Kingdom of Judah, he proposes that a careful reading of some psalms and of Proverbs allows

---

15. Carr, *Formation of the Hebrew Bible*, 472.
16. Younger, "Fall of Samaria," 470.

glimpses of biblical writing representing early interests of the monarchies of Israel and Judah. Overall, biblical psalms are quite difficult to date, and some (e.g., Ps 137) specifically reflect the Judean exile. But others, especially a sub-genre called royal psalms, use "archaic holdovers" that sound different themes than those in Torah and prophetic traditions.[17] "In your strength the king rejoices, O LORD, and in your help how greatly he exults!" proclaimed one (Ps 21:1). References in Proverbs underlined the role of royal scribes: "These are other proverbs of Solomon that the officials of King Hezekiah of Judah copied" (Prov 25:1). And borrowing from the thirty-chapter Egyptian Instruction of Amenemope, an Israelite scribe wrote for royal courtiers: "Have I not written for you thirty sayings of admonition and knowledge?" (Prov 22:20).

Like all the Hebrew scriptures, these psalms and poems are available only in manuscripts from the second century BCE and later. Both changing political and cultural norms eventually led to the copying of biblical manuscripts at Qumran and early Greek translations of the Torah in Egypt (see chapter 5). Yet without doubt some of the materials prepared by scribes for the rulers of Israel and Judah before they fell to Assyrians and Babylonians were later included in the biblical books. Because those monarchies did not survive, however, we must turn next to how the biblical story was upended and expanded when Jerusalem was destroyed and its rulers and scribes were deported to Babylon. It was there that exiled storytellers began collecting, editing, and copying their texts.

---

17. Carr, *Formation of the Hebrew Bible*, 401.

Chapter 3

How Do Archeological Findings Enhance the Bible's Backstory?

For both scholars and other curious readers, the reality that so little evidence for ancient texts from the earliest parts of the biblical story exists propelled hope that more evidence could be uncovered. In the 1980s the movie *Raiders of the Lost Ark* provided the popular view of how archeological discovery could affect modern life. In the movie, "good-guy" archeologists race to find the lost Ark of the Covenant before the "bad-guy" archeologists do, fearing that if it falls into the wrong hands its power will be used for destruction. Recent news illustrates continuing appetite for archeological evidence about the Bible as well as the quest for fame from the discovery of relevant ancient artifacts. For example, in 2020 it was revealed that a renowned scholar of ancient papyri, teaching at a prestigious university in Britain, had stolen fragments of ancient texts.[1]

Although the drama of the latest discoveries and research controversies in the eastern Mediterranean continues to attract an audience, trained archaeologists insist that their finds are mute, that is, never coming to the surface with explanatory labels attached.[2] So, contemporary readers may ask whether and how archeological evidence can help twenty-first-century readers to better understand the Bible's ancient story. McKnight proposes that: "The greatest contribution of archaeology . . . is not the confirmation or nonconfirmation of specific points. Rather, [it] uncovers the evidence

---

1. Moynihan, "He Taught Ancient Texts at Oxford."
2. Finkelstein and Mazar, *Quest*, 184.

HOW DO ARCHEOLOGICAL FINDINGS ENHANCE THE BIBLE'S BACKSTORY?

that enables scholars to reconstruct the conditions under which people lived in biblical times and to understand better the biblical world and faith that comes to expression in the biblical texts."[3] What, then, do we know about the biblical world and the faith of its authors? Describing the breadth and complexity of archeological data would take its own book; this chapter surveys only some of the well-known and at times controversial physical evidence related to the Bible.

The eastern Mediterranean has long been the target of archeological research. Naming this region, which covers Israel, Palestine, Jordan, Lebanon, Egypt, Turkey, and Greece, is complicated by the long history of European interventions in the region, as well as contemporary conflicts. From medieval crusades to the Holy Land, to nineteenth-century western military and political maneuvers, the places where the biblical stories emerged have also been regions for the assertion of European imperial power. Colonial control in the eastern Mediterranean also made it possible for many important archaeological discoveries to be made by Europeans, and many ancient artifacts are still curated in European museums. For example, the famous Egyptian Rosetta Stone stands in the British Museum.

From the mid-twentieth century to the present, archaeological research in the region has been tragically shaped by disputes that followed the formation of the State of Israel, and subsequent Israeli occupation of Palestine. Contemporary archeologists describe the region as Syro-Palestine, the Levant or the Holy Land.[4] Given the impact of ancient Egyptian empires on biblical accounts, Egyptian archeologists also provide information used by biblical scholars. And because New Testament texts also reflect regions in contemporary Turkey, Greece, and even Italy, archaeological research in those regions is also noteworthy.

In the early twentieth century, some scholars defined their work as the discipline of "biblical archaeology." Led by William F. Albright, excavators worked in Israel-Palestine with the hope of finding evidence for biblical accounts. The efforts of Christian Zionists to tie the modern State of Israel to the ancient Israelites also influenced archeological research. Today most scholars critique such approaches, and no longer refer to themselves as biblical archeologists.[5] Nevertheless, methods developed by these

---

3. McKnight, *Reading the Bible Today*, 56.
4. Dever, *My Nine Lives*, 190. See also Magness, *Holy Land Revealed*.
5. Dever, *My Nine Lives*, 189–90.

twentieth-century scholars, including excavation practices and dating methods, continue to shape more recent work "in the dirt."

Even the most optimistic of views about accurate dating for ancient biblical texts, however, cannot reach into the past uncovered by archeologists. Artifacts from the region are available from as long ago as the prehistoric Paleolithic period (25,000–10,000 BCE). The emergence of bronze technology corresponded with the emergence of historical documents in eastern Mediterranean region. Middle Bronze Age (2200–1550 BCE) artifacts are widespread, found on the coastal plain of modern Israel-Palestine, or biblical Canaan. Most scholars no longer claim that these materials directly illustrate the story of biblical patriarchs and matriarchs, but they acknowledge the importance of this evidence for understanding biblical thought. Some evidence from the Late Bronze Age (1550–1200 BCE) suggests that Canaanite culture declined during this time. Much twentieth-century research in Israel and occupied Palestine focused on later Bronze Age finds; even more relevant items related to the Israelite story come from the Iron Age (1200–586 BCE). The later centuries of this period can be cross-referenced with the stories of the monarchs and prophets of Israel and Judah, a cultural period that we have already seen as the time for the emergence of written texts in Hebrew. Ample archeological evidence is at hand reflecting the Babylonian destruction of Jerusalem in 587/86 BCE. Persian, Hellenistic and Roman rule of the eastern Mediterranean, from 539 BCE to 324 CE, is well documented through both historical documents and found artifacts.

The evidence from these periods, painstakingly analyzed, ranges from the grand to the miniscule. Tells, a key feature in the region, have provided much data for Israel-Palestine. The Hebrew word *tel* is translated in the Bible as "heap of ruins" (Josh 8:28). Visible on the landscape as massive mounds, tells are sites of human occupation over millennia, providing evidence that can be broadly dated. Workers record the layers they observe beneath the surface, based on geological and other evidence, a process known as stratigraphy. Archeologists also divide each layer into a grid as they dig, so that anything uncovered can be located by placement as well as level. Finally, they build retainer balks, or walls, around each grid so that later archaeologists can observe the layers that have been removed.

While both professionals and many interns who staff their digs dream of the "big find," everyone agrees that most archeological work is hot or cold, dusty, and painstakingly detailed. Items from the monumental to the miniscule are important. Material evidence such as walls and building materials, fire markings, figures/carvings, implements and decorative items, grave goods, and skeletal remains are uncovered and recorded. Architects and art historians also participate in the research. Geological phenomena such as earthquake damage may be visible within human structures. Organic matter such as seeds or wood offer dating possibilities. Among the most important pieces of archaeological data are pottery objects, usually in fragments called sherds. Pottery styles, ingredients in the clay, and levels at which sherds are found, are essential in the dating of other materials. Radiometric dating, which measures the carbon-14 isotope in organic materials, has been used in research since the beginning of the twentieth century.

Written characters, words, or longer inscriptions are equally significant. Throughout the region, large victory monuments, called stelae, praise the exploits of ancient rulers. The Merneptah Stela, uncovered in Egypt in 1896, is a granite slab over three meters high, describing the conquests of the pharaoh who ruled Egypt from 1213–1203 BCE. A few lines at the bottom refer to his campaigns in Canaan, including a hieroglyph that has been translated "Israel," in the declaration: "Israel is laid waste and his seed is not." This written text is the earliest reference outside the Bible to Israel as an identifiable people. While the text declares that Egypt has destroyed Israel, this phrase actually points to the emergence of an Israelite presence in the hill country of Judea.

Other archaeological sources include burial inscriptions, coins with both inscriptions and images, and, of course, manuscripts. Writing in the biblical languages of Hebrew, Aramaic, and Greek is found both on fragments and complete texts using the medium of papyrus or vellum, and even ostraca, or pottery sherds.

Computer and internet resources have dramatically changed the field of archaeology. Electronic sharing of research data, and careful study of specific items using digital photography and modeling, have enhanced understanding. Archaeometry, for example using electrochemical spectroscopes, has contributed new information regarding the types of food/substance residues found in pottery and clarifies the original locations, known as provenance, for clay or stone from which found items are crafted. Archaeologists can better understand human remains via bone-density scans, hair analysis, and dental records, revealing more about diet, disease, and life-expectancy.

Given the scale and diversity of evidence in the region, it is unsurprising that archeologists also disagree about how to interpret that evidence. The approaches of biblical scholars to archeological data in Israel, Jordan, and the occupied West Bank spread along a spectrum. Recognizing the significance of the Israelite monarchy in biblical accounts, maximalist scholars, who accept most of the biblical history as written near to the events it described, argue for the emergence of a powerful tenth-century monarchy under the rule of David and Solomon. At the opposite end are minimalists, who argue that the accounts in the biblical histories were developed by Jews much later than the history they detailed, during the Persian and Hellenistic periods.[6]

More nuanced interpretations of field data are of course possible, illustrating the range of both history and memory behind the biblical narratives. For example, the story of Joseph (Gen 37–50) describes him being carried as a captive to Egypt by traders in a camel train. Although Joseph's inclusion in Genesis includes him among Israel's patriarchs, most scholars place this story-within-a story as a later narrative. That perspective can be supported by records indicating that camels were domesticated much later.[7] Stories of the Israelite conquest include a list of thirty-one Canaanite kings (Josh 12:7–24), and Canaanite city states are well attested in second-millennium archaeological records. But most scholars agree that Joshua was composed later.[8] Having noted such gaps, many specific items and locations reveal intersections between archeological data and biblical accounts. Following are several examples of those intersections.

Tel Dan inscription: In 1993, Israeli archaeologist Gila Cook uncovered a stone inscribed in Aramaic at Tel Dan, in northern Israel. This stone was apparently a fragment of an unknown ruler's victory monument, dated to about 800 BCE; several fragments of this monument were later built into a wall that survived into modern times. In this inscription, the triumphant ruler claims that he killed a king who belonged to the House of David. The text is fragmentary, and researchers continue to study its original context. But the reference to the House of David in a monument indicates that Israel's rivals recognized an actual Davidic dynasty not long after his rule as described in the Bible. This discovery strengthened the perspective of those who assert that tenth-century King David was the historical king of a

---

6. Athas, "Setting the Record Straight," 241–55.
7. Finkelstein and Mazar, *Quest*, 46.
8. Finkelstein and Mazar, *Quest*, 64.

specific territory. The Tel Dan inscription further reports the killing of the "king of Israel," likely a son of Ahab (2 Kgs 8).

Mesha Stela/Moabite Stone: A second monument naming an Israelite ruler can be dated to the ninth century. According to the biblical record, Omri was king of Israel, and Omri's son Ahab was a major figure in the Israelite story (1 Kgs 17–22). The Mesha Stela honors Mesha, king of Moab, and praises his god Chemosh. Among Mesha's victories was one over the son of "Omri king of Israel." Other external historical documentation from the ninth century also indicated that the northern kingdom of Israel was more powerful and politically recognized than Judah, the smaller southern kingdom.

> 3.1 *The Palestine Exploration Fund, founded in 1865, was the oldest European-funded organization for the study of Palestine and Jordan. In its* Quarterly, *archeologists and other explorers published accounts of their work. In this segment from 1870, Anglican missionary F. A. Klein described his first visit to the Mesha Stela.*
>
> It was on the 19th of August, 1868, that in the course of a journey I undertook to Jebl Ajloon and the Belka that I arrived at Diban (ancient Dibon) about one hour to the north of the Wadi Mojeb (Arnon). . . . Carpets and cushions were spread in the tent of the Scheich, and coffee prepared with all the ceremonial of Bedouin etiquette. Before the operation of preparing and drinking coffee had been terminated, my friend Zattam, who was always most anxious to make my tour as pleasant and interesting as possible, had informed that there was among the ruins of Diban, scarcely ten minutes from our encampment, a most interesting stone with an ancient inscription on it which no one had ever been able to decipher, which he would take me to see. . . . I afterwards ascertained that his assertion as to no European having before me seen the stone was perfectly true; none of the distinguished travelers in those parts had ever seen or heard of it, or they would not have shunned trouble and expense to secure this treasure. . . . When I came to the spot where this precious relic of antiquity was lying on the ground, I was delighted at the sight, and at the same time greatly vexed that I did not come earlier, in order to have an opportunity of copying at least a good part of the inscription, which I might the under the protection of [my friend] Zattam have done without the least molestation. . . . The stone was lying among the ruins of Diban perfectly free and exposed to view, the inscription uppermost. I got four men to turn it round (it was a basaltic stone, exceedingly heavy) in order to ascertain whether there was no inscription on the other side, and found that

it was perfectly smooth and without any inscription or other marks. What time was left me before sunset I now employed in examining, measuring, and making a correct sketch of the stone, besides endeavouring to collect a perfect alphabet from the inscription.⁹

Inscribed stone storage jars: In the mid-1970s, Israeli archaeologists began work at a site in the Sinai Desert. One of their mysterious discoveries was three stone jars, dating to the eighth century BCE, which, when reconstructed, revealed both inscriptions and images. The inscriptions read "Yahweh and his Asherah." The images appear to represent an Egyptian deity. Scholars disagree on whether the words and the images are linked. But the words make clear that in some parts of ancient Israel people paired their god with a feminine deity. The word "asherah" in some form appears forty times in the Hebrew Bible, always as something or someone opposed by faithful Israelites (e.g., Exod 34:14; 2 Kgs 18:4). These stone jars offer a glimpse of ancient Israelite practice which corroborates the biblical texts that sharply criticize those exact practices.¹⁰

> 3.2 *William Dever, an American archaeologist who worked for decades in the eastern Mediterranean, described his 1968 encounter with a man who offered to sell an artifact likely stolen from an ancient tomb. This artifact provided another piece of information about ancient popular uses of Asherah.*
>
> In late October, as the fall rains were rapidly approaching, I was out in the field one day finishing a tomb drawing. An old man came along with a flat stone tucked under his arm, squatted down to smoke a cigarette, and finally spoke up, "Do you ever buy a *maktub* [an inscription]?" My ears perked up, but not wanting to drive up the price I continued to draw nonchalantly. In due course I said, "Sure." The old man said, "How much do you pay?" I paused, then declared, "We always pay two dinars" (about $7). He hesitated a bit, then said, "Tayeb" ("Good"). I scarcely dared to look at the dirt-encrusted stone but accepted it and laid it on the ground while I finished drawing. When properly cleaned and deciphered after much difficulty, the inscription read:
> (Belonging to) ʿUriyahu the governor;
> this is his inscription.

---

9. Klein, "Original Discovery," 281–83.
10. Smith, "God Male and Female."

HOW DO ARCHEOLOGICAL FINDINGS ENHANCE THE BIBLE'S BACKSTORY?

May 'Uriyahu be blessed by Yahweh
and saved from his enemies
by his Asherah.

I published this inscription . . . promptly but hesitantly in 1969–1970. Many years went by before mainstream biblical scholars recognized its far-reaching implications.[11]

Inscribed silver scrolls: In 1979, archeologists found two silver scrolls, one an inch and the other about four inches long. Uncovered in a Jerusalem tomb outside the Old City, these scrolls had apparently escaped the attention of tomb robbers from an earlier period. Unwinding the scrolls was a lengthy and delicate process, but led to great excitement when the inscription on the scrolls revealed the old Hebrew letters for the name of Israel's God, YHWH, and the words of what is known as the Priestly Blessing: "The LORD bless you and keep you" (Num 6:24). Since the scrolls can be dated to the seventh century BCE, this inscription is the earliest biblical writing currently available to us, dated about five hundred years before the Dead Sea Scrolls. These tiny scrolls may have been worn as amulets around peoples' necks, suggesting the significance of this blessing to ordinary people during the monarchy.[12]

Lachish letters: The city of Lachish was one of the few fortified cities in Judah outside Jerusalem. Excavations in 1935 uncovered a collection of ostraca at the city gate, containing letters sent to the military officials of Lachish during the last days before it fell to Babylonian forces in 586 BCE. The texts called on YHWH to support the requests of the writer, and described his desperation: "We are watching for the fire signals of Lachish according to all the signs which my lord has given, because we cannot see Azeqah" (see Jer 34:6–7).[13]

Documentation from Persian (500–300 BCE), Hellenistic (300–63 BCE), and Roman (63 BCE onward) periods shed light on how Jewish faith and identities developed between the return of Jews from Babylonian exile until the time of Jesus and Paul. Without doubt the most significant discovery of the twentieth century, from the perspective of understanding the biblical writings, was the discovery of the Dead Sea Scrolls in the Judean

---

11. Dever, *My Nine Lives*, 94–96.
12. Barkay et al. "Challenges of Ketef Hinnom," 162–71.
13. Ben-Tsiyon and Halpern, "New Light on Unknown Prophets," 23–25.

desert. Western explorers had visited the ruins at Khirbet Qumran since the mid-nineteenth century, but archeological interest in the ancient site exploded after thousands of fragments and scrolls, including biblical texts, were discovered in the late 1940s, in caves near Qumran. Chapter 5 will explore ways that research on manuscripts from the Judean desert has influenced both what is known about the ancient Hebrew biblical texts and how those texts shaped the biblical understanding of Jesus and his followers.

Galilee, the northern region where, according to the Gospels, Jesus lived during his youth, and for much of his public ministry, has also provided sites containing fascinating archaeological artifacts. In the 1980s, a drought around the Sea of Galilee brought to the surface the wooden framework of a boat, dated by radiometric methods to about the time of Jesus. Nothing specifically links the boat to Jesus or his disciples, but such a vessel recalls the Gospel stories about fishing and storms on the lake. In the same region, recent excavations in the Roman city of Sepphoris, close to Nazareth during Jesus's lifetime, are also of interest. Because Sepphoris was never mentioned in the Gospels, its excavation suggests more about how Galilean Jews could have interacted with the neighboring Roman colonial authorities. Its location so close to where Jesus grew up as the son of an artisan (Matt 13:55) has also led to the hypothesis that Joseph and Jesus might have worked on construction projects in Sepphoris.

Jerusalem has for centuries doubtless been among the most important archaeological sites in Israel-Palestine. Archeological research on the Temple Mount/Haram El-Sharīf, where the Dome of the Rock and the al-Aqsa Mosque are located, is strictly limited because of the deep significance of this location for Muslims, Christians, and Jews. Tragic violent clashes among believers from the three faiths have occurred at this site. Elsewhere in Jerusalem, excavations have unearthed parts of ancient walls, dating to the Hasmonean period, and in some cases possibly to the pre-exilic monarchy. Burial sites in Jerusalem, including rock-cut tombs from the Hellenistic period, have been carefully studied. Ossuaries, boxes where bones were collected after bodies decayed, also provide insights into first-century Jewish practices.

James ossuary: In 2002, a French scholar published an Aramaic inscription found on the side of an ancient ossuary that read: "James son of Joseph brother of Jesus." The excitement and controversy over this artifact became an international event. Two questions were raised: how to date the ossuary, and whether the inscription on the bone box was a recent forgery or a first-century etching. In 2003 the owner of the ossuary was arrested by Israeli authorities as a forger, but in a later trial his conviction was overturned. Most scholars have agreed that the ossuary represents first-century burial practices of Judean Jews. Some further point out that the names "James" and "Jesus" were used widely among Jews of that time, so that even if the inscription were ancient, it did not necessarily refer to the Jesus and James of the Gospels. Another essential question the ossuary raises for researchers is that of provenance, that is, where the artifact was first found. Since the James ossuary's provenance remains unknown, its significance is an unresolved matter. Scholars are rightly skeptical of items first brought to light by antiquities dealers or collectors rather than from accredited excavation sites.[14]

Church of the Holy Sepulcher: The Jerusalem of the New Testament, destroyed by the Romans in 70 CE, was completely rebuilt by Roman Emperor Hadrian in the early second century. Hadrian renamed the city in his own honor, and designated the region as Palestine. Hadrian also banned Jews, including Jesus believers, from his city. Thus, it is extremely difficult to know anything about whether and where members of the earliest communities of Christians remembered places associated with Jesus's life. But by the time of Roman Emperor Constantine, "Christians [had] marked and identified many of their holy places in Palestine."[15] Among those locations were sites identified as places where Jesus was crucified and buried.

The Church of the Holy Sepulcher is in a part of Jerusalem that had been outside the city walls at the time of Jesus, and Matthew's Gospel specifically referred to tombs outside the city (27:53). Excavations under the Church of the Holy Sepulcher have uncovered a quarry dating to the eighth century BCE, as well as remains of a pagan temple. On one of the ancient walls below the church, a Latin inscription and scratched graffito of a sailing ship likely represent efforts of early Christian pilgrims from the west to memorialize their visit to this holy site.[16] By the fourth century, pilgrims from around the Mediterranean began traveling to the Holy Land, seeking connections between biblical stories and their own lives. One such pilgrim described an Easter celebration at the church.

> 3.4 *The fourth-century pilgrim Egeria traveled from the western Mediterranean, and wrote a detailed account to her sisters at home. Egeria described her three-year pilgrimage to biblical sites in Egypt,*

---

14. Byrne and McNary-Zak, *Resurrecting the Brother of Jesus*.
15. Smith, "'My Lord's Native Land,'" 1.
16. Broshi, "Excavations in the Chapel."

> *Asia Minor, Persia, and Palestine, especially Jerusalem. In this segment she recounted Holy Week observances, including at the Anastasis, a church built over the smaller site (Martyrium) where Jesus was said to have been buried. The Anastasis was surrounded by the larger building now known as the Church of the Holy Sepulcher.*
>
> When the ninth hour [on Friday] is at hand, the passage is read from the Gospel according to Saint John where Christ gave up His spirit. After this reading, a prayer is said and the dismissal is given. [Later] everyone comes to the Anastasis and after they arrive there, the passage from the Gospel is read where Joseph seeks from Pilate the body of the Lord and places it in a new tomb....
>
> On the following day, which is Saturday, there is as usual a service at the third hour and again at the sixth hour.... Only one thing [during the Easter vigil] is done more elaborately here. After the neophytes have been baptized and dressed as soon as they came forth from the baptismal font, they are led first of all to the Anastasis with the bishop. The bishop goes within the railings of the Anastasis, a hymn is sung, and he prays for them. Then he returns with them to the major church, where all the people are holding the vigil as is customary.... After the vigil service has been celebrated in the major church, everyone comes again to the Anastasis singing hymns. There once again a text of the Gospel of the Resurrection is read, a prayer is said, and once again the bishop offers the sacrifice.[17]

These illustrations emphasize that the vast collection of archaeological data from Israel-Palestine and other ancient Mediterranean sites can indeed shed light on biblical records. Such research will continue and further discoveries will add to and nuance understandings of biblical stories and their background settings.

Yet, as we noted at the beginning, uncovered artifacts do not make biblical accounts true. They are valuable in themselves, revealing a bit of the richness and complexity of the times and places where people passed on and wrote down God's words. As the earliest followers of Jesus were urged to be "living stones" (1 Pet 2:5), people of faith today may ask first whether our choices and actions represent the God of the Bible, without whose divine love in the present anything revealed by ancient artifacts is of lesser worth.

17. Egeria, *Diary of a Pilgrimage*, 37–38.

Chapter 4

How Did the Scattering of the People of Israel and Judah Shape the Story?

Chapter 2 described how the rise of monarchy in Israel and Judah set the stage for written accounts that would become part of the Bible. Looking back on that period, the biblical historical books narrated how kings, and occasionally queens, came to rule. Prophets, proclaiming, "Thus says YHWH!" offered the Bible's theological response to the political choices of these monarchs. Although some debate the historicity of a unified kingdom under David and Solomon, scholars agree that by the late tenth century, the Israelite people had been split into recognized northern and southern kingdoms, called Israel and Judah.

In the eighth century BCE, prophets with powerful poetic voices arose, picking up the Mosaic role as spokespeople for YHWH. Even before these prophets became prominent, Israelites remembered Nathan, Elijah, and Elisha, who had confronted their political leaders with the word of YHWH. In the eighth century, the prophet Amos traveled from Judah to Israel to warn of the threat from Assyria, their powerful neighbor to the north. The book of Amos, although its composition history is complicated, is situated during the reigns of Israelite King Jeroboam II (786–746 BCE) and King Uzziah (783–742) in Judah. It reported that the prophet began to proclaim "two years before the earthquake," a temblor that scholars have dated to about 760 BCE (Amos 1:1). The prophet Amos roundly criticized wealthy Israelites, who, as external records indicate, were at the height of their economic power and political influence in the region. As he preached,

Amos also became the first biblical prophet "to be associated with a book that preserves his words."[1]

Hosea and Isaiah, eighth-century prophets who also cried out their critique, conveyed a message that shaped much of the rest of the Hebrew Bible. While the Torah recounted ancestral stories and the legal framework that God had set for their life, prophets emphasized how poorly the people had followed YHWH's laws or even remembered their own stories. "My people consulted a piece of wood," moaned Hosea, calling out Israelite idolatry (Hos 4:12). Isaiah exclaimed that God "expected justice, but saw bloodshed; righteousness, but heard a cry" (Isa 5:7).

Eighth-century prophetic voices were not envisioning an imaginary or distant future, but rather offering an astute assessment of both political and theological realities in the midst of more than a century of Israelite "experience of Neo-Assyrian domination."[2] By 721 BCE, the northern kingdom Israel had been destroyed by the Assyrians. Its people were deported, scattered throughout Assyrian territory, and a few fled south to Judah as refugees (2 Kgs 17). From then on, the prophetic word was largely Judahite. Hosea ended up as the only Israelite prophet quoted in the Bible. Those Israelite refugees who went to Judah carried with them their own stories and records of God's words, and their memories were woven into the ongoing proclamations of Judah's prophets.

The smaller kingdom of Judah managed to hang on for more than a century, juggling its alliances with Assyrians and Egyptians in an effort to resist rising Babylonian power. Judah's rulers, maintaining their Davidic identity, continued to record their deeds. In the mid-seventh century, Josiah was crowned king in Judah, ruling until 609. The Bible portrayed Josiah as a good king, who ordered that the temple be repaired. During the renovations, a "book of the law" was discovered by the high priest, who was apparently unfamiliar with this document. When the book's message was read to the king, he sent the high priest to the prophet Huldah, a woman who confirmed its message of divine judgment on his kingdom (2 Kgs 22–23). This account affirmed that the Bible's later editors knew of parts of the written Torah in writing during the monarchy.

Under Josiah the Babylonians began to threaten Judah, as well as broader Assyrian domination in the region. Josiah was killed by the Egyptian pharaoh while Egypt was moving to defend Assyria. Babylon's power

---

1. Devadasan Premnath, "Amos, Book of," in *NIDB* 1:135.
2. Carr, *Formation of the Hebrew Bible*, 338.

prevailed, however, and within decades they were demanding allegiance from the kings of Judah. These monarchs vacillated between falling in line and rebelling. Eventually, Nebuchadnezzar sent his armies to besiege Jerusalem, and in 597 the Judahite king Jehoiachin surrendered. The Babylonians stripped the palace and the temple, taking most of Jerusalem's elite into exile. They left another Davidic descendant, Zedekiah, to rule, but when he revolted, they returned in 587, captured Jerusalem, burned the temple, killed Zedekiah's sons, and led him to Babylon blinded and in chains (2 Kgs 24–25).

During Josiah's reign, the prophet Jeremiah began to preach, and he lived to see the destruction of Jerusalem (Jer 25:3). According to the book bearing his name, Jeremiah was carried off to Egypt by some Judahites who resisted his advice to surrender to the Babylonians. This book, available in two different outlines, one in Hebrew and one in the Greek translation, represented the chaos of the final years of the southern kingdom. Further, this account provided a sharp example of the oral and performative character of many biblical texts. According to scholars, "the community of performers [who passed on Jeremiah's message] ranged in time from perhaps as early as the last quarter of the 7th century to as late as even the 4th or even 3rd century BCE."[3]

Those who were exiled in Babylon must have carried with them scrolls containing the laws and stories that were important to them. Troubled that YHWH had allowed the destruction of the temple and the demise of the Davidic dynasty, scribes began to "gather and reframe" their ancient traditions "in light of experiences of exile."[4] Central to this self-examination, they spelled out a retrospective of all that had happened from Israel's arrival in Canaan until the Babylonian conquest. Labeled the Deuteronomistic History (DH) by modern scholars, this collection makes up a large part of the Hebrew Bible, from Joshua through 2 Kings. This collection of texts took the theological perspective of Deuteronomy as its point of departure. The blessings and curses of Deuteronomy pointed toward the histories' perspective that all Israelite and Judahite rulers were defined above all by whether they "did what was right in the sight of the LORD, and walked in all the way of [their] father David," or "did what was evil in the sight of the LORD, just as all [their] ancestors had done" (2 Kgs 22:2; 23:37). The DH

---

3. Louis Stulman, "Jeremiah, Book of," in *NIDB* 3:224.
4. Carr, *Formation of the Hebrew Bible*, 341.

also echoed the prophetic words of Jeremiah as well as earlier prophets, that God's punishment fell on those who did not observe God's law.

Other writings from the trauma of exile described the devastation experienced by the exiles. The poets of the book of Lamentations heaped up dirge-like recitals of Jerusalem as a weeping widow, their conquerors as brutal torturers and rapists, and their dismay that God had "become like an enemy" (2:5). The text of these laments was attributed elsewhere to Jeremiah (2 Chr 35:25), but probably reflected widespread cries of the exiles, perhaps even memories of the imperial aggression Judah had suffered even before it was destroyed.

Yet voices of prophetic hope were also raised from exile. In Babylon, a poet who was schooled in the teaching of the prophet Isaiah called out, speaking "tenderly to Jerusalem, and [crying] to her that she has served her term" (Isa 40:2). Later, Second Isaiah referred by name to the Persian general Cyrus, by then threatening Babylon, calling him the anointed of YHWH and promising to "go before you . . . for the sake of my servant Jacob" (Isa 45:1–4). Ezekiel, many of whose oracles are dated to specific events before and during the exile, envisioned a new temple, in the "twenty-fifth year of our exile" (Ezek 40:1).

Equally important for the exiles in Babylon, scribes began to collect, edit, and copy the many stories and laws that were central to their faith and their practices. Without a temple or a royal court to order written records, scribes and priests took on the task of forming a complete Torah. They clarified God's law according to ancestral tradition, in order to avoid future divine punishment for disobedience. As we discussed in chapter 2, modern scholars for many years tried to understand the process of the exilic scribes by segmenting out pre-Torah sources. Now, many scholars agree that, while the Torah revealed the influence of different traditions, the first five scrolls were founded on the weaving together two broad strands of ancient Israelite traditions. One visible indication of these two traditions can be observed in the two stories of creation in Genesis. The first story (Gen 1—2:3) is a liturgical recital of God's words and deeds. The second, beginning in Genesis 2:4, tells the story of God's forming of the earth creature Adam, thus opening the primeval saga that led to the blessing of Abraham in Gen 12. The first story is attributed to a group called Priestly writers, who studied the laws of Moses to define their worship practices in exile. The Priestly focus was also visible in detailed instructions for the wilderness tabernacle (Exod 25–31; 35–40). The second story rolled out the ancient accounts of the patriarchs and matriarchs of Israel, their enslavement in Egypt, and the entry into Canaan, leading eventually to the monarchy and the Deuteronomist's urgent call to apply God's covenant in a different political reality.

While exilic priests, scribes, and others in Babylon were copying these scrolls, their formal exile came to an end sooner than many had predicted. Within decades, Medo-Persian armies threatened Babylon from the east. Under their leader Cyrus, Persian policy toward subject peoples was expected to be different from that of their Babylonian rivals, so some exiles began to hope that they could soon return to Jerusalem. As recorded in the book of Ezra, YHWH "stirred up the spirit of Cyrus" to issue a proclamation of liberation and respect for the Jews (Ezra 1:1–2). The biblical account declared that Cyrus commanded the Judahites to return to Jerusalem and rebuild the temple of YHWH. Although this account is specific to the biblical witness, royal inscriptions from the time of Cyrus's rule in Babylon include a reference to his repatriation policy for deported peoples.

> 4.1 *The Cyrus Cylinder, a cuneiform document now in the British Museum, described the Persian general's conquest of Babylon (539 BCE). Cyrus presented himself as the perfect ruler, honoring Babylon's chief god Marduk, and ensuring the welfare of peoples that had been conquered by Babylon.*
>
> I took up my lordly abode in the royal palace amidst rejoicing and happiness. Marduk, the great lord, /established as his fate for me a magnanimous heart of one who loves Babylon, and I daily attended to his worship. My vast army marched into Babylon in peace; I did not permit anyone to frighten the people of [Sumer] / and\ Akkad. I relieved their weariness and freed them from their service. Marduk, the great lord, rejoiced over [my good] deeds. [In] peace, before [Marduk], we mov[ed] around in friendship. [By his] exalted [word], all the kings who sit upon thrones throughout the world, from the Upper Sea to the Lower Sea, who live in the districts [far-off], the kings of the West, who dwell in tents, all of them, brought their heavy tribute before me and in Babylon they kissed my feet.
>
> I returned the images of the gods, who had resided there, to their places and I let them dwell in eternal abodes. I gathered all their inhabitants and returned to them their dwellings. May all the gods whom I settled in their sacred centers ask daily of Bêl and Nâbu that my days be long and may they intercede for my welfare.[5]

---

5. "Cyrus Cylinder."

From Word to Book

The books of Ezra and Nehemiah described the first return to Jerusalem, in 538 BCE, and the prophets Haggai and Zechariah, during the 520s, encouraged the returnees who were struggling to rebuild the Second Temple. Ezra, "a scribe skilled in the law of Moses that the LORD the God of Israel had given" (Ezra 7:6), and Nehemiah, "a cupbearer to the [Persian] king" (Neh 1:11), picked up the account about a century later. The dates of their missions to Jerusalem are not certain, but both leaders returned with the permission of one of the Persian rulers. These two men were tasked with carrying out the prescriptions "in the law of Moses the man of God" (Ezra 3:2). Together with the Chroniclers (1–2 Chronicles), Ezra and Nehemiah represented the Priestly perspective. As they understood the Torah, Moses, the prophet without equal (Deut 34:10), had showed how to rightly read the ancient stories and interpretations of the law by later prophets and within the Deuteronomistic tradition.[6]

Meanwhile, however, biblical traditions also continued to be shaped through the lenses of people under Persian rule. The importance of Persian power and culture are visible in the words of Ezra, as well as in textual references to Persian kings. Aramaic, the language of the empire, appeared several times in the book (Ezra 4:8—6:18; 7:12-26).

The Persian period also provided settings where Jews began writing other stories. The book of Esther included details that showed the author's knowledge of the Persian world. King Ahasuerus, loosely based on Xerxes, (485-464 BCE), appeared in Persian records. Susa, the setting for Esther's story, was the winter administrative capital of the empire. Official Persian records revealed the wealth and pomp of the court (1:6-8), the empire's administration by a seven-member council (1:13-14), and the transmission of official messages across its territory by horseback couriers (8:1). The story of Esther acceding to the throne and her conquest of the evil official Haman cannot be corroborated historically, yet the account underlined realities sometimes faced by Jews in exile. The story also served as the foundation for the Jewish celebration of Purim, which in some aspects resembled a Persian festival.

Another fascinating text, the book of Tobit, also depicted the late Persian period. A story of exile, Tobit's Persian backdrop became clearer when the Aramaic text, which lay behind the known Greek text, was uncovered

---

6. Carr, *Formation of the Hebrew Bible*, 223–24.

at Qumran. Tobit was "both an adventure story and a moral tale," describing two families of Jewish exiles and the trials they underwent.[7] The book's characters, in the Jewish diaspora, traveled between Nineveh, capital of Israel's former Assyrian enemies, and Ecbatana, a city in Persia. The two families were faithful Jews, committed to carrying out laws of the Book of Moses. This identifying phrase, also found in the Hebrew Bible, appeared only in Persian-influenced works of Ezra, Nehemiah, and 1–2 Chronicles. Tobit's story exhibited concepts that revealed exilic influences, including the activities of angels. Disguised as a man named Azarias, the angel Raphael served as guide and mentor to Tobit's son Tobias.

> *4.2 At the end of Tobit, Raphael reveals himself to Tobit's family, with images that reflect later New Testament descriptions.*
> 11 "I will not conceal from you. I have indeed said, 'It is good to conceal the secret of a king but to reveal gloriously the works of God.' 12 And now when you and your daughter-in-law Sarra prayed, I brought the memorial of your prayer before the Holy One, and when you would bury the dead, I was likewise present with you. 13 And when you did not hesitate to get up and leave your dinner to go out and bury the dead, the good deed was not hidden from me, but I was with you. 14 So now God sent me to heal you and your daughter-in-law Sarra. 15 I am Raphael, one of the seven holy angels who present the prayers of the holy ones and enter before the glory of the Holy One." 16 Then they were both troubled, and they fell face forward, for they were afraid.
> 17 But he said to them, "Do not be afraid; you will have peace. But bless God forever. 18 For not by my grace, but by the will of our God have I come. Therefore, bless him forever. 19 All the days I appeared to you, but I did not eat or drink; rather, you were seeing a vision. 20 So now acknowledge God, for I am ascending to him who sent me. And write in a book all the things that have been accomplished." 21 Then they stood up, and they saw him no longer. (Tobit 12:11–21 *NETS*)

A non-biblical glimpse into Jewish faith and practice during the Persian period was found in a collection of Aramaic papyri uncovered in the nineteenth century from a settlement in Upper Egypt. These fifth-century BCE documents described many aspects of the life in a community of Jewish

---

7. Irene Nowell, "Tobit, Book of," in *NIDB* 5:612.

mercenaries defending the Persian Empire's southern border. The Elephantine collection, so called for the Greek name for the island of the settlement, included contracts, bills, and correspondence among Arameans, Persians, and Egyptians in this outpost. The texts did not include references either to the biblical patriarchs or to Moses. However, a document dated by its reference to Persian King Darius II (ca. 419 BCE), contained a letter from Hananiah, a Jewish authority serving in the Persian administration. Hananiah wrote "to my brethren Yedoniah and his colleagues the Jewish garrison" at Elephantine, giving instructions for the observance of a seven-day feast of unleavened bread.[8]

Thus, while little external evidence is available to show how theses texts were written, the texts themselves represent the editing and copying of Jewish writings during the exile and after the return. Such a process formed the Torah, and eventually the other writings that also were part of the Tanakh. In that same period, other Jewish writings also described people's hopes, fears, and quest for faithfulness. The categorization that eventually led to labels such as "canonical" and "apocryphal" was applied much later (see chapter 6). A fuller picture of early Second Temple experiences may elicit from readers a curious and generous interest in all the texts of this period.

> 4.3 *David de Silva, a professor of New Testament, is an expert on Jewish writings of the Second Temple period, in particular those writings known in most Protestant churches as the Apocrypha. In this essay, he argues for the importance of reading these writings.*
>
> The value of the Old Testament Apocrypha is not merely historical. These texts have not only informed people of faith but also have inspired them throughout the millennia. Many of the ethical ideals taken up by Jesus and his disciples and promoted in the New Testament find their roots here and so are reinforced and strengthened by the reading of them. But even more, these texts add fuel to the fire in the soul sparked and fed by the canon shared by all Christians. The zeal to walk faithfully with before God in the face of adversity, the commitment to choose obedience to God over succumbing to the passions or weaknesses of the flesh, the experience of God's forgiveness and expectation of God's deliverance—all these are strengthened by these texts, which one can approach with confidence at least as the best devotional literature to have withstood the test of time.[9]

---

8. Cowley, *Aramaic Papyri*, 60–65.
9. DeSilva, *Introducing the Apocrypha*, 40–41.

The next chapter turns to developments in the Bible's history that emerged in the Hellenistic period. Beginning with the conquest of the Greek ruler and military leader Alexander, the period that began in the late fourth century BCE and continued into the lifetime of Jesus provided a new language to express their thoughts and prayers, and more formal structures to create space for writing down their stories. While this new cultural setting sharply challenged their commitment to the God of Moses and the prophets, it also began to open a broader community to share their faith.

Chapter 5

How Did Jesus and His Community Enter the Story?

The world into which Jesus was born was rich in stories. His Jewish family must have heard many times how the Israelites were freed from slavery in Egypt, how Moses brought God's Torah to the people in the desert, how Samuel anointed David as Israel's king, and perhaps even how the prophetess Huldah warned Josiah of his kingdom's looming destruction. Jesus was born, most scholars think, about 4 BCE, during the reign of King Herod, a client ruler under the imperial control of Rome. By that time Jewish people had recited, collected, edited, and copied texts the Scriptures for centuries. Their scholars lived in Babylon, where many Jews remained after Cyrus had allowed many to return; in Egypt, where a large community had settled; in Asia Minor; in Galilee, and in Judea, which housed the temple. This Second Temple, rebuilt in Jerusalem by those who returned from Babylon, was a touchstone for Jews both in the diaspora and in Galilee and Judea. Herod the Great, to enhance his own reputation and to curry favor with Jewish religious leaders, greatly expanded this temple, the one whose destruction Jesus foretold, and which was demolished by Roman forces.

It is common to say that Jesus lived during the Second Temple period, a time beginning with the temple's reconstruction in 537 BCE and ending when Roman forces burned it in 70 CE. Most of the New Testament writings reflected on Jesus's life, death and resurrection from the perspective of those who knew the temple had been destroyed. Traditionally, many Christians have considered the time between the Babylonian exile and the birth of Jesus as a time when God was silent. Rather, as discussed in chapter 4, the Second Temple period was a time of lively theological reflection, storytelling, and biblical commentary among Jews.

Life in the eastern Mediterranean was dramatically disrupted when Macedonian general Alexander the Great burst onto the scene. Beginning his push eastward from Greece in 334 BCE, Alexander marched his armies east to the Indus River and south to Upper Egypt before his death in 323 BCE. In the process he upended Persian rule throughout the region, including asserting control over Galilee and Judea. A student of Greek philosopher Aristotle, Alexander believed in the superiority of Greek philosophy, language, science, and religion throughout the regions he conquered. Alexander's promotion of all things Greek was first of all to assure the communication of his far-flung armies, yet that hegemony reshaped most aspects of life throughout the territories he conquered. Jews as well as other peoples adopted a common trade language, Koine Greek, and what they wrote in both Aramaic and Greek articulated the challenges they faced as they responded to new cultural and political forces, sometimes resisting and at times assimilating.

Upon Alexander's early death, his territory was divided among his generals. Those who descended from the ruler Seleucus, known as Seleucids, ruled the region called Syria, including Galilee and Judea, while the descendants of Alexander's bodyguard Ptolemy, the Ptolemies, took control in Egypt. Jews, in experiences that echoed the stories of the Israelites centuries before, were caught between these two competing dynasties. In the early years after Alexander's death, Jerusalem and its surroundings were controlled by the Ptolemies, but in 198 BCE the Seleucids defeated them and took control. This political change deepened struggles among leaders in Jerusalem, some siding with the Seleucids and others retaining loyalty to the Ptolemies. Some Judean Jews were also more open to Hellenistic practices, while others resisted them.

During this time writers looked back on their experiences under Persian domination and tried to grasp their new realities. The biblical book of Daniel, whose central figure steadfastly observed the Torah in the courts of Babylon and Persia, was one account of the struggle for faithfulness. A portion of Daniel (2:4b—7:28) is written in Aramaic, the language of the Persian Empire. Later, the visionary declared that what he saw began with the last four kings of Persia, yet continued the beastly metaphors he had introduced when he described the arrival of Greek forces: "The ram . . .

with the two horns, these are the kings of Media and Persia. The male goat is the king of Greece" (Dan 8:20–21).

Another book from this period, the Wisdom of Ben Sira, also known by its Greek title Sirach, included eight poems about wisdom. Sirach concluded with a poem in honor of the Jerusalem high priest Simeon (142–134 BCE). Originally in Hebrew, the work was translated into Greek by Ben Sira's grandson, likely in Egypt. For Ben Sira, the personified figure of Wisdom who spoke in Proverbs, who had been present at creation, had then taken residence in the temple in Jerusalem.

> *5.1 Ben Sira built on the earlier description of creative wisdom in Prov 8, portraying how wisdom came to reside in Jerusalem.*
> 1 Wisdom will praise her soul,
> and in the midst of her people she will boast.
> 2 In an assembly of the Most High she will open her mouth,
> and before his power she will boast:
> 3 "I came forth from the mouth of the Most High,
> And like a mist I covered the earth . . .
> 8 "Then the creator of all commanded me,
> And he who created me put down my tent and said,
> 'Encamp in Iakob, and in Israel let your inheritance be.'
> 9 Before the age, from the beginning, he created me,
> and until the age I will never fail.
> 10 In a holy tent I ministered before him,
> and thus in Sion I was firmly set.
> 11 In a beloved city as well he put me down,
> and in Ierousalem was my authority.
> 12 And I took root among a glorified people,
> in the portion of the Lord is my inheritance." (Sirach 24 *NETS*)

In 175 BCE the Seleucid Antiochus IV Epiphanes ascended to the throne in Syria and began a brutal campaign to suppress faithful Jewish practices. In response, a priestly family from a village outside Jerusalem revolted. The well-known account of their struggle, which led to the expulsion of the Seleucids and the cleansing of the Jerusalem temple, which Antiochus had profaned, are detailed in 1–2 Maccabees.

> *5.2 The Book of 1 Maccabees opened with the conquests of Alexander the Great, then recounting the story of Jewish resistance against Antiochus. This segment described the beginning of the revolt led by*

the priestly family of Mattathias, eventually led by his son Judah, known as the Maccabee (the Hammer). From this nickname the revolt became known as the Maccabean Revolt.

44 And the king [Antiochus] sent documents carried by the hand of messengers to Ierousalem and the cities of Iouda to follow precepts foreign to the land 45 and to withhold whole burnt offerings and sacrifice and libation from the holy precinct and to profane sabbaths and feasts 46 and to defile holy precinct and holy ones, 47 to build altars and sacred precincts to idols and to sacrifice swine and common animals 48 and to leave their sons uncircumcised, to make their souls abominable in every unclean and profane thing, 49 so as to forget the law and to change all the statues. 50 And whoever would not abide by the command of the king would die.

15 And the agents of the king, who were enforcing the apostasy, came to the city of Modein to sacrifice. 16 And many from Israel came to them, and Mattathias and his sons gathered together. 17 And the agents of the king answered and said to Mattathias, saying, "You are a ruler, both glorious and great in this city, and supported by sons and brothers. 18 Now you come forward first and execute the ordinance of the king, as have done all the nations and the men of Iouda and those remaining in Ierousalem. And you and your sons will be among the Friends of the king, and you and your sons will be glorified with silver and gold and much compensation." 19 And Mattathias answered and said with a loud voice, "If all the nations which are in the realm of the king obey him so as to apostatize, each one from the religion of their fathers, and adopt his commandments, 20 both I and my sons and my brothers will walk in the covenant of our fathers. 21 God help us if we abandon the law and the statutes; 22 we will not obey the words of the king nor deviate from our religion to the right or to the left." (1 Macc 1:44–50; 2:15–22 *NETS*)

Within a few years, members of the Maccabean family had taken up roles as high priests in Jerusalem, and soon proclaimed themselves monarchs as well. Despite resistance to foreign rule based on Torah-faithfulness, this family's inclination toward monarchy revealed their assimilation of some aspects of hellenization. Some Jews resisted the moves of the Maccabean family, which soon established itself as the royal house of the Hasmoneans, likely a reference to an ancestor. Yet, again echoing the environment that had given rise to the earliest biblical texts, the formation of a royal house also created an environment that could further develop and stabilize written biblical texts.

The rise of the Hasmonean dynasty also supported the development of other literature celebrating resistance to foreigners together with Torah observance. For example, the book of Judith portrayed a courageous, beautiful, and faithful widow who engineered the defeat of Israel's enemies by subterfuge. Judith, from an unknown village somewhere outside Jerusalem, confronted the army of Assyrian general Holofernes on his way to desecrate the temple. The writer signaled that the work was fiction by naming the enemy king Nebuchadnezzar, who had ruled Babylon after that empire's defeat of Assyria. Judith, reminding readers of the ancient biblical women of valor, Deborah and Jael, seduced Nebuchadnezzar's general into drinking too much when she was invited to his tent, then cut off his head. Along with the Maccabean texts, the book of Judith, available only in a Greek text, was not part of the collection that eventually became the Tanakh. Yet the dramatic figure of Judith became one of the most represented biblical women in Western art.

Other Jewish writers were also active during the Hellenistic period. Their writings are now referred to as pseudepigrapha because they often adopted the pseudonyms of ancient Israelite characters. The literature included retellings of Torah, for example Jubilees, a reframing of Genesis; apocalyptic visions, for example 1 Enoch, named after the ancient Enoch of Gen 5; the Thanksgiving hymns of Qumran, and moral exhortations like the Testaments of the Twelve Patriarchs. While the Hasmonean monarchy provided the platform for standardizing texts and shaping what materials would be widely read and copied, the diversity of scrolls found at Qumran revealed that some Jews during this period did not restrict or formally categorize what they read and copied.

Meantime, in the Jewish diaspora, hellenization meant that faithful Jews came to need the Scriptures in Greek. Although Alexander had boasted that he had conquered territory from India to Ethiopia, the primary impact of his hellenization policies in the centuries after his wars was experienced in the eastern Mediterranean. The Septuagint, the Greek translation of the Hebrew Torah, dramatically witnessed to the widespread hellenization of Jews (see chapter 2).

Yet the translation of the Jewish Scriptures from the Hebrew language into Greek signaled something new. While ancient victory monuments or treaties also had religious underpinnings, the sacred texts of the Jews had been copied, edited, and collected by people who were not rulers, but rather placed at the bottom of ancient empires. Jews took their name from their homeland, Judea, but for centuries they had also lived from Babylon to Asia Minor and Egypt. Biblical history and prophecy often reflected sharp criticism of monarchy, their own and those of their powerful neighbors, in light of the covenant that YHWH had made with their ancestors. Yet as the result of Greek conquest, many Jews, especially outside Judea, were no longer able to understand their scriptures in Hebrew.

Another upheaval shook Jews in the eastern Mediterranean as Roman imperial power spread. Disputes among the Hasmonean rulers attracted the attention of expansionist Roman leaders, leading to military action, and Roman general Pompey took over Judea in 63 BCE. For a time, Hasmonean monarchs maintained a semblance of control in their territory, but Herod, ruler in neighboring Nabataea, negotiated with the Romans a role for himself, fully taking the Judean throne in 37 BCE. Herod married a Hasmonean princess, Mariamne, in an effort to gain Jewish support, but Jews always considered him an outsider. Further, Herod exhibited his personal concerns as well as his attitude toward Jews when he later executed Mariamne and two of their sons, fearing that she and her children threatened his rule.

Roman colonial power in this tiny province on the edge of their empire continued to manipulate the differing political perspectives among Jewish leaders. Those conflicts also reflected different understandings among Jews about what the Scriptures said about God's world and their place in it. Apart from the century of independence under Hasmonean rule, Jews in Palestine had been subjected to imperial forces from the time of Assyrian domination, through the Babylonian exile, Persian rule, and finally Seleucid control. By the time the New Testament writers began composing their letters, sermons, and stories about Jesus, faithful Jews had struggled for a century with Roman ways of colonizing and exploiting them.

Within that setting, first-century Jewish historian and Roman client Josephus described four "philosophies" among Jews: Sadducees, Pharisees, Zealots, and Essenes. While the term "philosophy" would have made sense to his pagan readers, modern readers might be better able to understand these groups as schools of thought. Among the differences that shaped these Jewish groups was their approach to interpreting the Scriptures, some of which were noted in the New Testament. Sadducees administered the Jerusalem temple and assured observances of the prescribed festivals and offerings. Biblical conservatives, they accepted only the five books of Moses as authoritative. As Jerusalem's religious and economic elites, Sadducees were also the party that negotiated with the Roman overlords and, in the Gospel accounts, the authorities who handed Jesus over to Pilate.

Pharisees were reformers. When Paul described his early life (Phil 3:5), he underlined how seriously Pharisees took the Scriptures. Like Jesus, Pharisees used new interpretative methods to bring biblical texts alive in their own contexts. Jesus, though, differed from the Pharisees on how to preserve ritual purity, as in his story about the Pharisee and the tax collector (Luke 18). Pharisees were open to new theological proposals, and Luke described Paul playing on that fact when he named belief in resurrection to incite an argument among Sadducees and Pharisees at his trial (Acts 23).

Zealots followed the revolt tradition of the Maccabees. While Zealots did not play a visible role in the New Testament, their point of view was referenced in the speech by the Pharisee Gamaliel (Acts 5). And their insistence that they would give their loyalty to God alone, in accord with the earlier Maccabeans, justified taking up arms against the Romans. The life of Josephus offered one picture of interactions between Sadducees and Zealots, as he was both of a priestly family and a military leader during the Jewish revolt against Roman rule from 66–70 CE.

Essenes, named as Josephus's fourth school, are not mentioned in the New Testament. Essenes were righteous Jews who shared possessions, lived simply, some of them celibate, strictly observed the Sabbath, and practiced regular ritual washing.

> *5.3 Josephus, a Jewish general, surrendered to a Roman general late in the Jewish revolt, and predicted that the general's family would ascend to the Roman throne. From Rome, Josephus wrote books detailing Jewish history and explaining Jewish beliefs and practices for his patrons. In this segment, he described the Essenes, likely the group to which the Qumran community belonged.*
>
> 122 Since [they are] despisers of wealth—their communal stock is astonishing—, one cannot find a person among them who has more in terms of possessions. For by a law, those coming into the school must yield up their funds to the order, with the result that in all [their ranks] neither the humiliation of poverty nor the superiority of wealth is detectable, but the assets of each one have been mixed in together, as if they were brothers, to create one fund for all.
>
> 129 After [their early morning prayers], they are dismissed by the curators to the various crafts that they have each come to know, and after they have worked strenuously until the fifth hour they

are again assembled in one area, where they belt on linen covers and wash their bodies in frigid water. After this purification they gather in a private hall, into which none of those who hold different views may enter: now pure themselves, they approach the dining room as if it were some [kind of] sanctuary. 130 After they have seated themselves in silence, the baker serves the loaves in order, whereas the cook serves each person one dish of one food. 131 The priest offers a prayer before the food, and it is forbidden to taste anything before the prayer; when he has had his breakfast he offers another concluding prayer. While starting and also while finishing, then, they honor God as the sponsor of life. At that, laying aside their clothes as if they were holy, they apply themselves to their labors again until evening.[1]

Most scholars think that members of the Essene community, angered by what they viewed as the corruption of Hasmonean rule, withdrew to the desert near the Dead Sea sometime during the second century BCE. When, in the mid-twentieth century, a large collection of scrolls and manuscript fragments were discovered in caves near the ancient settlement known as Khirbet Qumran, scholars quickly connected these astonishing finds with ancient accounts about Essenes. The scrolls offered new information about the world into which Jesus was born, and thus reports that trickled out from scholars analyzing the scrolls led to speculation about how their findings might change what was known about Jesus and the emergence of the Christian movement. Whatever their importance for understanding Christianity, however, the Dead Sea Scrolls, whose publication began in 1951, above all provide astonishing perspectives on the breadth of biblical knowledge and theological reflection of diverse Jewish communities under Roman control.

The Qumran scrolls named the community who copied and hid them the Sons of Zadok. This reference back to the high priestly family of David and Solomon provided their claim to ancient legitimacy. Likely their withdrawal to the desert and their repudiation of Jerusalem leaders also shaped their self-description as a faithful remnant called "the poor," and "the Sons of Light." Qumran texts provided glimpses into the community's history, laid out the rules for their communal life, and pronounced their prayers and praises. Other texts found in the caves were among those that modern scholars label pseudepigrapha. Still others are works now included

---

1. Josephus, *Jewish War*, in *Flavius Josephus*, 2.8.2–5.

in biblical canons, including at least portions of all of the Old Testament books except Esther. However, nothing in the finds at Qumran indicated that the community had categorized their scrolls according to modern labels. Although Torah observance and priestly rules within that law were central to their community, the Qumran residents also wrote down their own constitution for living together.

Before the first Qumran scrolls were discovered in 1947, modern Bibles were translated from Hebrew using a set of medieval manuscripts known as the Masoretic Text (MT). The most prominent of these manuscripts was made in Cairo in 1008 and is the oldest complete manuscript of the Hebrew Bible. The fragments and manuscripts from the Dead Sea region, some dated as early as two hundred years before the time of Jesus, thus provided a much longer and older textual history for the Hebrew Bible. Because they were copied in a time close to the first translations into Greek of Scripture, they now make it possible for scholars to consider different text traditions used by ancient Jews. According to one scholar, "The Qumran findings provide an important starting point for Pentateuchal exegesis and corroborate the legitimacy of critically using MT in Pentateuchal research."[2] Another Qumran expert notes that among the Isaiah scrolls found at Qumran, one was virtually the same as the later Masoretic Text, while another Isaiah scroll had many text variations. However, this study also indicated that the later Masoretes did not seek to make their own theological points, finding no "sectarian variants" in the Hebrew of the medieval codices.[3]

Among the Qumran community's manuscripts was one describing their vision of a coming war that, under God's direction, they would take up against the "children of darkness." This War Scroll, as well as some Qumran biblical commentaries, reflected a community that had not only withdrawn from broader society, but also eagerly awaited the enactment of God's final plan for history, God's complete victory over religious corruption and political oppression. Such apocalyptic imagery had been part of the expression of earlier hopes of faithful Jews. Similar apocalyptic images had already been used in Daniel, with visions that were both historically based and full of metaphorical images. For first-century Jews, God's plan included liberation from Roman domination and return to rule by those anointed by God. That hope also shaped the first communities of

---

2. Schmid, "Who Wrote the Torah?," §11.
3. Ulrich, "Our Sharper Focus," 12.

HOW DID JESUS AND HIS COMMUNITY ENTER THE STORY?

Jesus's disciples. Jesus, however, taught something different about the use of violence (Matt 26:52–54), and apocalyptic battles portrayed in Revelation showed the victory of God's word rather than weapons (Rev 19:13–15).

Other aspects of life at Qumran were also similar to New Testament portraits of Jesus and his community. The Qumranites shared property and ate a common meal; as biblical interpreters they read the Hebrew prophets as describing their own times, much like Matthew, who frequently quoted Scripture as fulfillment (e.g., Matt 2:15). Further, as the Gospels quoted Isa 40 to describe the location of John the Baptist's ministry, Qumran texts explained their move with the prophet's words, "In the desert prepare the way of the Lord." Some scholars think that John the Baptist lived for a time at Qumran, especially since the location where he began to baptize was very close to Qumran. Still, the ministries of John the Baptist and Jesus reflected differences from Qumran practice. Full members at Qumran needed to be males who practiced priestly purity laws, while John the Baptist and Jesus included both women and men who did not or could not practice ritual purity.

Although historians have unearthed much information about the world where Jesus was born from Qumran texts, New Testament writings still provide the most intimate portraits from those who knew Jesus and his first disciples. In contrast to the long period of emergence of the Old Testament, the Christian New Testament developed over barely one century. Jesus, an itinerant preacher who never wrote anything, lived during the first third of the first century CE. During the second third of that century, stories of and preaching about Jesus spread beyond Galilee and Judea. By the last third of the century, Jesus's followers were writing down his words and deeds to explain how Jesus was God's Messiah, based on their reading of Scripture.

The earliest records about Jesus available to us are the first-century letters of the apostle Paul, written about twenty years after Jesus's lifetime. Paul did not know Jesus firsthand; rather, he encountered the risen Jesus in a vision that turned him around, from persecuting the Jesus community to proclaiming Jesus as God's Messiah. Paul provided few details of that encounter, but acknowledged that he later spent time with the disciple Peter and Jesus's brother James (Gal 1–2). Paul also insisted that eyewitnesses to Jesus's resurrection were still alive as he wrote (1 Cor 15:6), but made few references to Jesus's life, apart from the brief comment that he was "born of a woman" (Gal 4:4).

On the other hand, Jesus's crucifixion and resurrection were central to Paul's gospel. For him, these events revealed that God had indeed ushered in the new age awaited by Jews influenced by apocalyptic hope. Paul anticipated its completion would come with the near return of Jesus Christ. In one place, Paul used the same images that Jesus had, when Jesus spoke of his return: angels, trumpets, and the gathering up of God's people (1 Thess 4:16–7; Matt 24:30–1). At the same time, Paul also argued that Jesus's followers should live rightly in the "in-between" times, also echoing Jesus's words (Rom 14:13; Matt 7:1). Paul sometimes directly quoted Jesus, most notably when Jesus offered bread and wine to the disciples just before he died (1 Cor 11:23–5; see Luke 22:17–20 and parallels).

For perhaps thirty years, Paul traveled widely throughout the eastern Mediterranean region, proclaiming the good news of Jesus to the nations, or gentiles, as Jews knew them. At the heart of his message was that Jesus, whose title Christ, from the Hebrew Messiah, he regularly used, had revealed God's plan for all creation. Yet Paul was far from the only messenger of God's historical inbreaking. Indeed, he clarified that he had reached an agreement with Peter and James that he would preach to the gentiles while they would proclaim Jesus to Jews (Gal 2:9–10). Because believers soon collected and circulated Paul's many letters, however, the profile of his mission significantly shaped the New Testament and the story of the earliest churches.

Paul admitted that a crucified Messiah was a scandal to Jews, and others of Jesus's disciples also struggled to make sense of what happened to their leader. As a Pharisee, Paul had likely participated in his group's conversations about the idea of resurrection before he became a follower of Jesus. Yet crucifixion, in Greco-Roman culture, was the horrifying punishment for terrorists, and the idea of bodily resurrection did not make sense to many of them. Paul had to write a long explanation about resurrection to his Corinthian converts (1 Cor 15), and emphasized that resurrection was the vindication of Jesus's crucifixion (Phil 2:5–11).

Likewise, resurrection accounts in the Gospels did not mask the complexity of their claims. The Gospel of Mark stated that the women who encountered Jesus's empty tomb fled out of fear (Mark 16:8). In Matthew, the evangelist asserted that at Jesus's final resurrection appearance, "some doubted" (Matt 28:17). Thus, while Jesus's stories, teaching, and mighty deeds were discussed and remembered, the shocking drama of Jesus's crucifixion and resurrection were most likely the first events that his followers discussed, puzzled over, and wrote down. Mark, the Gospel that many consider the earliest written account of Jesus's ministry, spent half of the text describing the last week of Jesus's life, his crucifixion and resurrection. The apostolic foundation of Mark's account was soon attested by theologians and historians as they linked his story to the testimony of the disciple Peter.

> 5.3 *Eusebius, a fourth-century bishop of Caesarea in Palestine, produced a* History of the Church. *In this segment, Eusebius quoted an earlier bishop, Papias, on the significance of the apostle Peter. Papias was a second-century bishop of Hierapolis, in modern Turkey.*
>
> Papias, however, in the [introduction] of his works does not indicate that he was an eyewitness or hearer of the holy apostles at all, but teaches that he received the matters of the faith from those who had been familiar with them.... And he presents other accounts of the words of the Lord as being from ... the presbyter John. We direct lovers of learning to them, but at present we must include along with the words of his that have already been set down a tradition that he has recorded about Mark the evangelist, in these words: "And the presbyter used to say this, that Mark was Peter's translator, and he wrote down accurately, though not in order, what he remembered [hearing] about what the Lord had said and done. For he had not heard the Lord or been his follower, but later, as I said, was Peter's. Peter used to teach using short examples, but he did not compose an ordered account of the Lord's sayings, with the result that Mark did not err in writing the particulars he remembered. For he took forethought for one thing, not to falsify or omit anything of what he had heard in the accounts he wrote."[4]

Apostle Peter played a prominent role in all four Gospels, as well in Paul's few autobiographical notes. Perhaps illiterate, Peter was nevertheless an important leader in the earliest days of the Jesus movement and a source for firsthand information. The fact that all the Gospels were honest about Peter's character flaws pointed to this apostle as a credible source. It was also significant that all four Gospels reported women as the first witnesses to Jesus's resurrection. Luke's Gospel recorded that when the women witnesses told others they had seen Jesus alive, the "[apostles] did not believe them" (24:11).

The four Gospels, written most likely in the final third of the first century, are not biographies of Jesus (see 5.4, below). Yet Matthew, Mark, Luke, and John, all soon recognized as authoritative for followers of Jesus, shared the same broad storyline: after baptism by John the Baptist, Jesus began a public life of teaching and healing, came into conflict with religious authorities, was

---

4. Eusebius, *History of the Church* 3.39.14–15.

crucified by soldiers under the authority of the Roman governor Pilate, and appeared in a resurrected body. Recording these accounts and expressing their theological impact mattered more and more as the early disciples died. In addition, the Jesus community, as well as other Jews, was scattered after the Roman destruction of Jerusalem, making written records more important.

While the Gospels record much about Jesus's life and teaching, however, they were above all written to persuade audiences that Jesus was God's Messiah and God's Son. The Gospels were also written as two-level accounts. At the first level they recounted stories about Jesus, a man from an unremarkable Jewish village in backwater Galilee, where small agriculture and artisanry were means of survival. At the second level, they appealed in Greek to a wider urban audience throughout the Roman Empire, following Jesus's death and resurrection.

The Gospels also reported much more about what Jesus said than noted in Paul's few citations. Jesus was an excellent storyteller, expressing himself memorably in ways that could be repeated. These sayings and longer teachings were copied in the Gospels, sometimes where one Gospel was a source for the others, and at times representing traditions about Jesus handed down orally among his followers. Jesus's proclamation about the imminence of God's reign was repeated in Mark, Matthew, and Luke. John's Gospel also emphasized entering God's realm, observing this concept from another angle (3:3, 5). The parable about a farmer who sowed seed that produced in different quantities appeared in Mark, Matthew, and Luke (Mark 4 and parallels). Jesus's conversation with a rich young man was also recounted in all three Gospels (Mark 10 and parallels). A much larger body of teachings of Jesus was included in Matthew and Luke, with closely comparable phrases that probably represented an earlier written collection of Jesus's sayings. Scholars refer to this collection as Q, or the Sayings Source. Central teachings such as the Beatitudes (Matt 5; Luke 6) or parables such as one about a shepherd searching for one lost sheep (Matt 18; Luke 10) are familiar to many. Matthew and Luke, however, also included material unique to each of them, most notably their nativity stories (Matt 2; Luke 2).

John presented Jesus's words in a different way than the other three Gospels. For example, he included lengthy meditations by and about Jesus that reflected the concerns of second-generation disciples of Jesus (see John 14–17, 21). John also described Jesus's ministry over a three-year period, including multiple visits to Jerusalem. Many scholars think this longer ministry account is a credible record, making it much more likely that

Jerusalem authorities were well aware of who Jesus was before the Passover when he was arrested.

Some sayings of Jesus appeared elsewhere rather than in the Gospels. For example, Paul's farewell sermon to the Ephesians, in Acts, cited Jesus's claim: "It is more blessed to give than to receive" (20:25). One of the most beloved stories about Jesus, that is his response when the authorities brought to him a woman caught in adultery, now appears in most Bibles in the Gospel of John just before chapter 8. Yet the story was copied in other places in a variety of early Gospel manuscripts. This story apparently circulated separately, and scribes who found it a credible account of Jesus's teaching retained it even when it was not easily located in one Gospel location.[5]

Soon other Christian writings also were given the label "gospel." While all of these texts represented reflections by Christians on how Jesus fit into the divine economy, they did not parallel the straightforward narrative and memorable teaching in the four Gospels that were later canonized. The Gospel of Thomas, found in a Coptic version among the manuscripts discovered at Nag Hammadi in Egypt in 1945, has attracted particular scholarly interest. This manuscript can be compared to the earlier Sayings Source/Q, because it included sayings of Jesus that parallel those in the four Gospels. Some think that the Gospel of Thomas represented one of the earliest records of Jesus's sayings, because a few Greek fragments of Thomas were known before the Coptic version was discovered. However, the Gospel's introduction suggests something else: "These are the hidden words that the living Jesus spoke and Didymos Judas Thomas wrote them down." Thomas can be contrasted to the four Gospels, both in its claim that what Jesus said was secret and by naming its disciple-author.

By the end of the first century, Paul's letters were apparently known as a collection. In fact, one letter writer both referred to these letters in the plural, and compared them to the "other Scriptures" (2 Pet 3:16). So, although Paul wrote letters, first of all as advice to his churches and as commentaries on the Scriptures in light of Jesus Christ, his letters quickly gained a different status. Texts of the Gospels likewise might have been addressed to particular communities of Jesus followers, but they were soon understood as written for all the churches, and belonging together. Together, letters attributed to Paul, the four Gospels, and Luke's sequel Acts make up more than 80 percent of the New Testament. Other disciples also wrote about who Jesus was and why he mattered, and these writings were eventually

5. Knust and Wasserman, *To Cast the First Stone*.

included in the New Testament. The next chapter will discuss how the New Testament canon was formed, as used in almost all churches. Here, however, we have observed the groundwork being laid for the claims that the story of Jesus Christ changed everything, both for those who walked with him and those who attended to their preaching. According to their reports, many people experienced that change as good news.

> *5.4 New Testament scholar Raymond Brown (1928–1998) published several volumes outlining the historical background for the birth and the death of Jesus. Here Brown responded to questions about how theology and history interact in the New Testament.*
>
> Only in a limited way is Christianity "a religion of the book." Those who followed and proclaimed Christ existed for some twenty years before a single NT book was written (i.e., before AD 50). Even when the NT books were being composed (*ca.* AD 50–150), Christian communities existed in areas where no preserved book was authored; and surely they had ideas and beliefs not recorded in any NT book. . . . Furthermore, during the last few decades in which NT books were being penned, Christians were producing other preserved writings (e.g., *Didache, 1 Clement,* Epistles of Ignatius of Antioch, *Gospel of Peter, Protoevangelium of James*) . . . . [This book concentrates] on the twenty-seven books accepted as the canonical NT. Such a concentration is legitimate because they have had a uniquely normative place in Christian life, liturgy, creed, and spirituality. Moreover, these books exist, and in that sense are more certain than conjectural, undocumented, or sparsely documented reconstructions of early Christianity. . . . We do not have exact reports composed in Jesus' lifetime by those who knew him. Rather what we are given pertinent to the life and ministry of Jesus comes to us in a language other than the one that he regularly spoke and in the form of different distillations from years of proclamation and teaching about him. In one sense that attenuated reminiscence might seem an impoverishment; in another sense, however, the Gospels understood in this way illustrate how Christians, dependent on word of mouth, kept alive and developed the image of Jesus, answering new questions.[6]

---

6. Brown, *Introduction to the New Testament,* viii–ix.

Chapter 6

What Are Biblical Canons, and How Were They Formed?

Exploring the long history of the Bible that we have considered so far, for many readers, next raises questions about how the Bible's contents were determined. We have learned how people of faith had, for centuries, been reciting and writing down their experiences of God and their reflections on those events. Some of those stories and experiences, eventually in writing, provided the foundation for the liturgies and daily life of Jewish communities in the ancient Mediterranean. Yet those communities continued to experience God's presence, or wonder about what God was doing, or pray and praise God, while those written texts were taking shape. So other literature beyond core texts like the Torah also told stories of faith. How did all those writings, developed over a long time and a wide geographical spread, become one Bible? Some scholars describe this process as "the paradox of double-agency, creaturely and divine."[1] More skeptical readers assume that purely human processes of choice and exclusion were at work.

It is a statement of faith to declare that God's Spirit was active in the process of forming the biblical canon, and learning more of the story can help to shape that claim. So, this chapter surveys the "creaturely," human, aspects of the Bible's formation. Questions to consider include what is known about how the biblical texts were chosen, when they were chosen, and who chose them. Christians and Jews who approach the Bible with a sense of trust often find that learning more about the process of building a

---

1. Metzger, *Canon of the New Testament*, 285.

canon deepens their understanding of divine guidance in the process. Some are more skeptical, finding it more realistic, and certainly more dramatic, to envision clusters of powerful men, gathered in back rooms, deciding what to keep and what to discard. Perhaps they even had swords in hand! In either case, it is nevertheless essential to admit that, over centuries, the vast majority of biblical readers have agreed on the worth of most of the texts in the Bible's pages, and have retained them for their life-giving wealth.

The root meaning of the Greek word *canon* describes a measuring rod of a fixed length. By extension, the term has evolved to describe the criteria, whether practical or metaphorical, by which any item can be evaluated. Although the Latin derivative *canon* became the term for written records of church councils, what might today be called "minutes," the use of "canon" began to be applied to biblical text lists only in the eighteenth century. The Greek word *graphe*, or "writing," was a much earlier term used by Jews, and the related phrase "it is written" often signaled biblical citations.

As described in chapters 4 and 5, Hebrew and Greek-speaking Jewish communities studied their core texts to define belief and practice, centuries before Jesus and his disciples began their ministry. In Hebrew, and then in Greek translations, the Torah/Pentateuch, or Book of Moses, held pride of place. Genesis, Exodus, Leviticus, Numbers, and Deuteronomy, although they included many different kinds of writing, were named Torah because they told the story of God who created everything, revealed God's name YHWH, and gave the law to Moses.

Chapter 4 described the exile of Judahite leaders to Babylon in the late sixth century BCE, and how that trauma catalyzed the collecting, editing, and copying of the Torah. It is difficult to date all the literature formed then and during the return of exiles to Judea. But both Ezra and Nehemiah, in the fourth century, reflected clearly worded commitment to the law of Moses as they encouraged and challenged the returnees. Both post-exilic leaders recorded events when they carefully observed what "they found ... written in the law, which the LORD has commanded by Moses" (Neh 8:14; see also Ezra 6:18). Over the next few centuries, the Torah and texts collected as a grouping called "prophets" shaped a more formal Jewish identity.

> 6.1 *In 132 BCE, the grandson of Jeshua Ben Sira penned an introduction to his grandfather's wisdom poems. In this prologue, the grandson, as he translated his grandfather's work, referred several times to a formal collection of his ancestors' "great teachings." In this*

WHAT ARE BIBLICAL CANONS, AND HOW WERE THEY FORMED?

excerpt, the younger author formally labeled two collections that became part of the Tanakh, and refers more generally to the writings.

Seeing that many and great things have been given to us through the Law and the Prophets and the others that followed them, for which reason it is necessary to commend Israel for education and wisdom, and whereas it is necessary that not only those who read them gain understanding, but also that those who love learning be capable of service to outsiders, both when they speak and when they write, Iesous, my grandfather, since he had given himself increasingly both to the reading of the Law and the Prophets and the other ancestral books and since he had acquired considerable proficiency in them, he too was led to compose something pertaining to education and wisdom in order that lovers of learning, when they come under their sway as well, might gain much more in living by the law. (Prologue to Ben Sira, *NETS*)

The Gospels, written entirely in the first century CE, also referred to the collected writings used by Jesus and his followers.[2] Luke's Gospel twice quoted Jesus's teaching from "Moses and the prophets" (Luke 16:16; 24:27). At one place, Luke added that Jesus also referenced the psalms (24:44). Although it is useful to cast a broad net in considering what writings were in use by first-century Jews, including Jesus, New Testament references to Scripture are not easy to count. For example, Jesus could have been remembering Isaiah's promise that God would prepare a great feast (Isa 25:6) when he described the banquet of the coming kingdom of heaven (Matt 8:11). However, we can count more than seventy times when the New Testament noted that Jesus or others cited texts with the phrase "It is written." New Testament writers quoted frequently from the psalms, the prophet Isaiah and, in the Torah, Deuteronomy, Genesis, and Exodus.

Other first-century Jewish writers who quoted Scripture identified their core collection as having a "fixed number." Josephus set this number at twenty-two, and while he did not list the titles he included, he emphasized that his collection began with the five books of Moses.[3] Another Jewish writer, using the pseudonym Ezra, referred to twenty-four books "that everyone can read," suggesting that he also knew of additional writings (4 Ezra 14:44). Most scholars think that books described here included the

---

2. Some scholars date a few New Testament texts to the early second century.
3. Josephus, *Against Apion*, in *Flavius Josephus*, 1.37–42.

same works as those on Josephus's list. For Jews the Bible's fixed number became known by the Hebrew term for "reading," as used when the scribe Ezra had gathered the returnees in Jerusalem: "So they read from the book, the law of God, with interpretation. They gave the sense, so that the people understood the *reading*" (Neh 8:8, my emphasis).

Historians used to think that, after the destruction of Jerusalem, near the end of that century, a gathering of Jewish rabbis established the authoritative biblical canon. However, recent analysis of ancient rabbinic debates is more nuanced. Over time, the rabbis recorded their debates, with specific notations regarding the books of Esther, Song of Songs, and Ecclesiastes/Qoheleth. One report in the Mishnah, from the third century, assured readers that "all holy scriptures defile the hands." Yet this claim was followed by a series of statements where different rabbis underlined disputes about Qoheleth or the Song of Songs. One scholarly proposal is that the rabbis were aware of and troubled by the absence of the Divine Name in all three of these texts. That proposal seems reasonable, since, so far, no fragments of Esther have been identified in the Qumran documents. And when Esther was translated into Greek, references to God were added. But it is likely that the descriptor of texts that "defile the hands," which ironically is a positive idea, had to do with matters of protocol such as how scrolls should be unwrapped. In any case, one scholar insists, the twenty-two texts that became known as the Tanakh, were "simply accepted. . . . No one ever canonized them."[4]

The rabbis also spent time debating how to categorize Ben Sira, whose prologue (see 6.1 above) had pointed toward a defined biblical collection. Still, second and third century Jewish texts never quoted from any of the Jewish writings that eventually formed the Deuterocanon/Apocrypha. Another Second Temple work insisted on the priority of the prophets for faithful Jews, who during this time awaited the arrival of the new prophet that Moses had promised long ago (1 Macc 4:46, 14:41; Deut 18:15). Clearly the Torah and the texts known as the Prophets were central to early Jewish understandings of Scripture. Because some of the psalms and collected proverbs were probably very early Israelite writings, later wisdom texts such as Ben Sira could have been viewed as commentary on the Torah.[5] And although these writings were later included in Christian Bibles,

---

4. Barton, *History of the Bible*, 219–21.
5. Chapman, *Law and the Prophets*, 289.

scholars such as the translator Jerome regarded them as "edifying although not scriptural."[6]

Chapter 4 named several other writings from the Second Temple period that portrayed Jewish faith and experience, yet also were not considered as part of their Bible. In addition to the priority of the Torah and the Prophets, many of these later texts were available primarily or only in Greek. By the second century CE, Jewish scholars had begun to prepare different Greek translations of the Bible, because of disagreements over how the Jesus movement had claimed the earlier Septuagint. Since in Jewish liturgy Scripture was still copied and read from scrolls, another explanation for the limitation on biblical titles could have been practical—fewer scrolls were easier to store or transport.

During the second century, a collection of commentaries by Jewish scholars, known as the Mishnah, was taking shape. This "'Teaching' [was] compiled by Rabbi Judah the Prince around the end of the second and the beginning of the third century CE. Rabbi Judah is best described not as the author of the Mishnah but as its editor, since he used earlier collections and other early material, often leaving these in their original form in his compilation."[7] The understanding of authoritative texts within Jewish communities, rather than concentrating on formalizing the "reading," evolved into the idea that the Torah could be written or oral, with the Mishnah as a first portion of oral Torah. "All the later teachings of the sages and teachers of Israel are embraced by the Oral Torah, seen as a continuous process."[8]

Emerging as a messianic movement among Galilean and Judean Jews, Jesus's community based their preaching on Scripture, both citing specific texts and referencing a broader written collection. As we saw in chapter 5, the first written records of this community were the letters from Paul, a Hellenistic Jew from Asia Minor. Offering advice and counsel to his churches, Paul frequently quoted Scripture in Greek. He was interpreting the texts he knew very well, sometimes using rabbinic methods and sometimes drawing on Hellenistic philosophical conventions. As frequently as Paul quoted Scripture, he also alluded to scriptural themes as he spelled out how being "in Christ" should be expressed in practice. For example, the entire argument of his letter to the communities in Rome was built upon the concept

---

6. Barton, *History of the Bible*, 226.

7. Jacobs, "Mishnah," in *Concise Companion*.

8. Jacobs, "Oral Torah," in *Concise Companion*.

From Word to Book

of the righteousness/justice of God which was so prominent throughout the prophets.[9]

Paul wrote to urban communities of Jesus's followers, many of them gentiles, scattered around the Aegean Sea. Meant to be read out loud, Paul's letters gave a vivid picture of the itinerant teacher praising, cajoling, or scolding the communities he had founded. This correspondence is referred to as "occasional," since it was addressed to specific problems, or "occasions," in local communities. At first, these letters were not understood as Scripture; yet the apostle certainly intended them to represent his authority among his churches. Paul also brought to the fore the Greek term *evangelion* (gospel) to define his message about Jesus. Paul's letters also showed that teachings of and stories about Jesus were widespread within decades of Jesus's death. At times he cited teachings as a "word from the Lord," (1 Cor 7:10), and at key points emphasized traditions from Jesus that had been handed down to him (1 Cor 11:23–26). Elsewhere he echoed Jesus's teachings known from the Gospels (Rom 12:14).

After Paul's letter-writing campaign, the Gospels laid out their proclamation about Jesus the Messiah. The shared outline of Matthew, Mark, and Luke offered one broad narrative arc. As noted in chapter 5, similarities among Jesus's sayings, whether short proverbs or longer teachings, pointed to very early transmission of Jesus's words. Moving into the second century, theologians throughout the Mediterranean world began to refer to Jesus's teachings in ways that further affirmed traditions from Jesus that they received and passed on.

The use of the word "gospel," or *evangelion*, for a written account of Jesus's life and teachings emerged in the first century. The earliest gospel in the New Testament opened with the proclamation: "The beginning of the gospel of Jesus Christ, the son of God" (Mark 1:1).[10] Mark's usage of "gospel," a term in Greco-Roman culture for reports of imperial and military triumphs, pointed to a Roman audience for his account. But the triumph for the evangelist, rather than imperial conquest, was the good news that "the reign of God has come near" (Mark 1:15, author's translation). Thus, it appears that the writer used "gospel" to describe the content, rather than the genre, of his story about Jesus.

---

9. Hays, *Echoes of Scripture*.

10. While not all scholars agree that the Gospel of Mark is the earliest gospel, this theory is widely held.

WHAT ARE BIBLICAL CANONS, AND HOW WERE THEY FORMED?

In the second century, Justin Martyr, a gentile Christian philosopher who was executed about 160 CE, described writings about Jesus as "memoirs of the apostles." Irenaeus, a Greek-speaking leader from Asia Minor who became a bishop in Gaul/France, was the first theologian known to list the four Gospels together by name (ca. 180–200). Tatian, a Syrian student of Justin, edited an early form of the four Gospels into a single text, or a harmony, titled the Diatessaron, "by means of four." This work, translated into Syriac, Arabic, Armenian, Georgian, and Latin, showed that many Christians thought of the writings about Jesus as four in number. At the same time, the editing of the Diatessaron made clear that written texts of the Gospels were still fluid enough that it was deemed appropriate to shape them in specific ways.[11]

By the late second and early third centuries, the Gospels were circulating as a collection, evident from Egyptian papyri manuscripts discovered in the nineteenth century. Although fragmentary, these collections were collected in codices, an early book format bound between covers. Codices containing Pauline letters were also found among the Egyptian papyri. For educated ancient Mediterranean people, scrolls had long been the desired medium for important writing. Although the codex was easier to handle and pass along, scholars demonstrated their expertise and erudition by how they found their place in the scrolls. Among Christians, codices functioned as less formal notebooks, quite likely as memory aids for itinerant Christian teachers.[12]

Beyond Gospel and Pauline letter collections, lists prepared by ancient Christian teachers began to name other writings that they used. Marcion, a second-century mariner and theologian, rejected the entire collection of Jewish Scriptures, and for his churches chose only the Gospel of Luke and Paul's letters. Rather than trying to formalize a canon, however, Marcion seemed motivated by his desire to cut churches' ties to Jewish communities. Although Marcion was condemned by Justin Martyr and Irenaeus, some churches who accepted his teaching survived for several centuries. In contrast to Marcion and his followers, during the third century, Origen wrote commentaries on both Old Testament books *and* several Gospels. So, Origen's work was one sign that Christians had come to consider the newer texts as having a similar scriptural character as the older ones.

---

11. Koester, *Ancient Christian Gospels*, 37–43, 243–44, 403–4.
12. Carr, "Rethinking the Materiality," 594–621.

One early New Testament list named twenty-four accepted New Testament books. Called the Muratorian fragment after the eighteenth-century scholar who discovered it in a monastery library, this fragment has been dated to the late second century, but some scholars think it is from the fourth century. Because of its fragmentary nature, the names of the Gospels in the Muratorian document must be filled in, although they are assumed to be the four Gospels that Justin and Irenaeus accepted. The Muratorian list also included the thirteen letters attributed to Paul, but not Hebrews, James, 1 and 2 Peter, and 3 John. Whatever its date, the Muratorian fragment apparently meant to inform readers about the texts the churches were using rather than outlining a prescribed list.

By the fourth century, however, it is clear that churches were paying more careful attention to which New Testament writings they affirmed or hesitated over. Such clarity became essential early in the Diocletianic/Great Persecution of 303–11, when throughout the Roman Empire Christians were ordered to hand over their "inspired and sacred writings" to be burned.[13] Not long after that, Roman rulers proclaimed religious toleration and an end to persecution of Christians. By 325 CE, the Christianized emperor Constantine called a council to deal with a conflict among Christians about how to define the divinity of Jesus Christ. Traditionally modern writers have placed the final formalizing of the New Testament to this Council of Nicaea, and identified Constantine as enforcer of this decision. Yet the records of the council are murky at best, and the canons of the council published later did not include a list of approved books. Likewise, the credal statement written at Nicaea continued to be a matter of hot debate throughout Christian communities for decades.

Eusebius of Caesarea, fourth-century bishop and church historian, had attended the council at Nicaea, and later became a key source for what happened there.

> 6.2 *In this segment of his* History of the Church, *Eusebius discussed how the churches viewed New Testament texts. He placed the texts into three categories and further emphasized apostolicity as essential for inclusion.*
>
> The holy quartet of the Gospels must, of course, be placed first. The writing of the Acts of the Apostles follows them. And the letters of Paul are reckoned after it. And it must be considered proper to place the first letter that bears the title "of John" and likewise

---

13. Eusebius, *History* 8.2.

the first "of Peter" next after them. After them must be placed, if it seems right, the Apocalypse of John, the [variant] opinions concerning which we will include at the right time. These are among those that are acknowledged [as genuine].

But of the writings [whose authenticity] is disputed, but are well known to many, there are in circulation the so-called letters of James and Jude, a second letter of Peter, and those letters termed the second and third of John; they belong either to the evangelist or to another with the same name as he.

Let be tallied among the illegitimate writings the Acts of Paul, the work called the Shepherd, and the Apocalypse of Peter, and in addition to them the letter bearing the title "of Barnabas," and the so-called teachings of the apostles, and also, as I said, the Apocalypse of John, if it seems right, which some, as I said, reject, but others judge it to stand among the writings accepted [as genuine].[14]

Eusebius's reference to the fourth-century debate over Revelation/Apocalypse of John merits attention. His historical collection had included correspondence from the Alexandrian bishop Dionysius, who challenged Revelation's inclusion in the New Testament. Dionysius's argument, now widely accepted, was that the apocalyptic author could not be the same writer as the author of John's Gospel, assumed to be an apostle, because of the differing vocabulary and syntax in the two texts.

By the fourth century, another kind of evidence for inclusion of New Testament texts appeared, when several large Bibles in codex format were copied. The most famous of these, Codex Sinaiticus, became known to Europeans when a nineteenth-century explorer encountered it in a monastery in the Sinai Desert.[15] This particular codex, in Greek, had by then lost many of its Old Testament pages, but 2 Esdras, Tobit, Judith, 1 and 4 Maccabees, Wisdom and Sirach/Ben Sira were present. Happily for modern scholars, Sinaiticus included the twenty-seven New Testament books now part of Roman Catholic, Orthodox, and Protestant canons, and also two other early Christian works. Both of these, Shepherd of Hermas and the letter of Barnabas, had been labeled by Eusebius as illegitimate. Other complete Bible codices from this period included the four Gospels, Acts, and the

---

14. Eusebius, *History* 3.25.

15. The complete manuscript of Codex Sinaiticus, together with translation, can be viewed online at https://www.codexsinaiticus.org/en/codex/.

Pauline letters. Codex Vaticanus did not have 1 and 2 Timothy, Titus, and Revelation, while Codex Alexandrinus added the Psalms of Solomon, a Jewish text from the first century BCE, and two second-century letters written by Clement, the bishop of Rome.

In 367 CE, Athanasius, bishop of Alexandria, wrote to the Egyptian churches to set the date for that year's Easter festival. In this letter, Athanasius exhorted them to read the twenty-two books of the Old Testament, using Josephus's enumeration. He further listed the twenty-seven books now common to most New Testament canons, describing this collection as: "fountains of salvation, that they who thirst may be satisfied with the living words they contain."[16] An identical New Testament list was included in the canons of the Council of Carthage in 397. This document also recommended that "the church over the sea be consulted to confirm this canon," an indication of important relationships between North African churches and churches as a much broader geographical community.[17]

This overview the first four centuries of the Christian movement demonstrates that no single theologian, council, or ruler, ordered and established the list of New Testament writings that would from then on be accepted by all Christians. Still, the fourth-century experience was definitive for recording what are now called canon lists. Several factors shaped this process over those early centuries. First, texts were included because they were widely both used and found useful. As seen in the papyri fragments, broad acceptance was foremost for the four Gospels and the letters of Paul. The high regard for the four Gospels and the Pauline letters may also have been indicated by their placement at the head of the lists, perhaps mirroring the position of the Torah and the Prophets in the Old Testament. So, church leaders and councils, rather than imposing those texts on their churches, were naming texts that were widely honored.

Second, for early churches the apostolicity of texts was essential. While the apostolic names given to the Gospels are not found within the Gospels themselves, the ancient traditions of the church connected these works directly to Jesus's disciples. Mark, according to several second-century Christian theologians, was the recorder of Peter's memories and teaching. In some cases, apostolic links were part of some communities' acceptance of texts, but did not persist more broadly. Thus, for example, the popular Shepherd of Hermas could have been understood as a reference to a friend

---

16. Athanasius, *Letter* 39.4–6.
17. Westcott, "Codex Canonum Ecclesiae Africanae," 18.

WHAT ARE BIBLICAL CANONS, AND HOW WERE THEY FORMED?

Paul mentioned (Rom 16:14). As noted above, Hermas was included in the Codex Sinaiticus, but excluded by Eusebius.

A third criterion for inclusion in New Testament lists was their alignment with what theologians called "the rule of faith," or "the rule of truth." The word used for this criterion was "canon." While no one rule was in print for everyone, several New Testament texts pointed toward its content (1 Cor 8:6, 15:3–4; Matt 28:19). Irenaeus clarified in debates with other Christians that "the church, though spread throughout the world, received from the apostles and their disciples" a faith based on belief in one Creator God, and in Jesus Christ "who became flesh for our salvation."[18] As parts of the Bible were copied and circulated throughout the churches, the rule of faith provided a sounding board against which any texts they heard could be evaluated. A final and mostly practical criterion for inclusion, among Christians, was the collection of biblical writings as codices, and thus under one cover.

As the Christian movement spread, churches from Baghdad to Ethiopia to Europe both translated the Bible and continued to evaluate the texts they used. Among churches who read the Bible in Greek, often called eastern churches, medieval records include at least "six different lists of the Scriptures of the Old and New Testaments." Many early eastern missionaries were Syriac-speaking Christians. Biblical manuscripts in Syriac have been found in Lebanon, Egypt, Sinai, Iraq/Iran, Armenia, India, and China, some of which omitted 2 Peter, 2 and 3 John, Jude, and/or Revelation.[19]

In Europe, after centuries of disagreements over both theology and practice, the Council of Florence (1442) failed in its effort to reunite eastern churches with the church in Rome, but affirmed the same New Testament list as Athanasius and the Council of Carthage. Still, in sixteenth-century Europe, theologians whose work impelled the Protestant Reformation continued to resist the inclusion of several New Testament books.

> 6.3 *German reformer Martin Luther, in the prologue to his 1522 German translation of the New Testament, gave high praise to Paul's letter to the Romans as "the purest gospel." Throughout he emphasized that criterion as well the importance of apostolic authority.*
> In a word, St. John's Gospel and his first Epistle, St. Paul's epistles, especially Romans, Galatians and Ephesians, and St. Peter's first epistle are the books that show you Christ and teach you all that it is necessary and salvatory for you to know, even if you were never

---

18. Irenaeus, *Against Heresies* 1.10.1.
19. Metzger, *Canon of the New Testament*, 217–18.

to see or hear any other book or doctrine. Therefore St. James' epistle is really an epistle of straw, compared to these others, for it has nothing of the nature of the gospel about it.

About this book of the Revelation of John, I leave everyone free to hold his own opinions. I would not have anyone bound to my opinion or judgment. I say what I feel. I miss more than one thing in this book, and this makes me to consider it to be neither apostolic nor prophetic.

Finally, let everyone think of it as his own spirit leads him. My spirit cannot accommodate itself into this book. For me this is reason enough not to think highly of it: Christ is neither taught nor known in it. But to teach Christ, this is the thing which an apostle above all else is bound to do.[20]

In Europe, debates about canon lists rose to the fore as scholars began to translate the Bible from Hebrew and Greek, instead of or alongside the Latin Vulgate. Luther chose to translate the Old Testament into German using the Hebrew Masoretic Text, thus pointing reformers away from books in Greek such as Tobit and the Maccabean books, read in churches for centuries, and known as the Deuterocanon. Protestants called those texts the Apocrypha; although that term originally meant "hidden," it developed the connotation of being false. In response, the Roman Catholic Council of Trent in 1546 declared an anathema of all those who did not accept "as sacred and canonical the said books entire with all their parts, as they have been used to be read in the Catholic Church, and as they are contained in the old Latin vulgate edition."[21]

Today, both Jews and Christians read from all the books known as the Tanakh or the Old Testament. Christians, however, vary in their use of the deuterocanonical or apocryphal writings. The twenty-seven New Testament books first listed in Athanasius's correspondence are affirmed in most Christian churches, while some churches in the Syrian Orthodox tradition do not include 2 John, 3 John, 2 Peter, Jude, and Revelation in their lectionary. The Ethiopian Tewahedo Church includes eighty-one books in its canon, including some writings specific to its own historical setting. Comparative canon lists are widely available in electronic sources to be pondered by everyday readers.

20. Luther, *Prefaces to the New Testament*, 362, 398–99.
21. Waterworth, *Canons and Decrees*, 19.

From time to time, ordinary readers as well as scholars have proposed the possibility of adding other writings, either ancient or more recent, to the biblical canon. Discoveries such as that of ancient codices at Nag Hammadi in Egypt in 1945 make some wonder whether new information about Jesus might still be uncovered, potentially changing traditional Christian teachings. Modern calls to repentance, such as Martin Luther King's "Letter from a Birmingham Jail," remind readers that the central message of Scripture resounds faithfully in other times and places. Across the centuries, believers have both continued to read the Bible and to record their own experiences of and prayers to God. Rather than trying to include or exclude more texts from what would now clearly be a human-derived list, it is well worth the effort to read the Bible in conversation with other theological, artistic, and scholarly texts. Many have found these intersections valuable and challenging, and conversations among modern readers greatly enrich what biblical canons teach.

> 6.4 In Katie's Canon, *womanist theologian Katie Geneva Cannon described how her family, drawing on the traditions of their enslaved ancestors, both embodied and interrogated the biblical canon.*
>
> In essence, spirituals were the indispensable device that slaves, forbidden by slaveholders to worship or, in most cases, even to pray, used to transmit a worldview fundamentally different from and opposed to that of slaveholders. For instance, slaveholders spoke of slavery being 'God-ordained' while slaves sang 'O Freedom! O Freedom!' . . . The spirituals express my ancestors' unflinching faith that they, too, were people of God. As spiritual singers, slaves were not bothered by the chronological distance between the biblical era and their present. Operating on a sense of sacred time, they extended time backward so as to experience an immediate intimacy with biblical persons as faith relatives. In other words, the characters, scenes, and events from the Bible came dramatically alive in the midst of their estrangement. The trials and triumphs of Noah riding out the flood, Moses telling Pharaoh to let God's people go, Jacob wrestling all night with an angel, Daniel being delivered from the lion's den, Shadrach, Meshach, and Abednego walking in the midst of flames, Joshua fighting the battle of Jericho, and Jesus praying in the Garden of Gethsemane are some of the Bible stories my foreparents committed to music as they interpreted their own experience against a wider narrative of hope and courage.[22]

---

22. Cannon, *Katie's Canon*, 35–36.

Chapter 7

How Did the Bible in Spanish Develop?

The first question in this book considered the implications of reading ancient documents in translation. Each Bible version that has been prepared, whether centuries ago or recently, has its own story. Readers of the Bible in English can access a variety of accounts of the work of translators like the medieval philosopher John Wycliffe and his students; William Tyndale, burned at the stake for his translation; and the committee who rendered the famous King James Version. This chapter tells a story less well known, although even older than the story of the English Bible: the story of the Spanish Bible. Although Spanish speakers live throughout the US and Canada, as well as form the majority of people in Central and South America, many North Americans do not grasp the significance of this heritage in their neighborhoods, let alone around the world. According to one study, "Spanish is the 2nd most spoken native language after Mandarin Chinese, and the 4th most spoken language overall after English, Mandarin, and Hindi."[1] And while the story of the Bible in Spanish, like the English Bible, begins in Europe, its beginnings can be traced to fourth century Palestine. Throughout, the Bible in Spanish is also remarkable because of how it was shaped by Jewish biblical scholarship and encounters with Muslims.

The peninsula that on modern maps includes Spain and Portugal was at the western limit of the Roman world, yet was influential throughout the Mediterranean. Already in the first century, the apostle Paul declared this region as the ultimate goal of his mission: "I desire, as I have for many years, to come to you when I go to Spain" (Rom 15:23). Paul used the

---

1. Wood, "How Many People Speak Spanish?," §3.

Greek word *Spania*, a geographical term used earlier by Phoenicians and Carthaginians. Ancient geographers also sometimes called the peninsula Iberia, and that word became the Roman label for the region. From the beginning of Roman rule, Iberian culture, language, and political systems had an important impact on Rome. Two second-century Roman emperors were Spanish, and a third-century Christian bishop, Hosius of Cordoba, served as advisor to Constantine, the first Roman emperor to be baptized as a Christian. Emperor Theodosius (347–395 CE), who declared Nicene Christianity the official religion of the empire, was also born in Spain. Despite Theodosius's declaration about Nicene Christianity, however, Iberia was ruled for more than a hundred years by Visigoth-Germanic emperors who ascribed to Arian Christianity. Arian Christians defined the divinity of Christ differently from the Nicenes, based on different interpretations of New Testament statements about Jesus.

The fact that Iberian and Roman societies were closely related meant that Old Latin Bible translations circulated quickly in Spain. The Old Latin version began to be replaced in the fourth century with the translation prepared by Jerome, a Roman biblical scholar who spent his later years as a monk in Bethlehem. Licinius, a Spanish theologian, wrote to Jerome, requesting him to send to the west copies of both original and translated biblical manuscripts. Two letters written by Jerome recorded their conversation, one to Licinius, in 398 CE, and one a year later to Licinius's wife Theodora. After Licinius's death, Theodora continued to be part of a study group working with these sacred texts.[2]

By the year 600, distribution of the Latin Bible as a complete book, rather than portions of the Bible, often the collected Gospels, was the norm. Archbishop Isidore of Seville frequently quoted Jerome's Latin version in his commentaries and biblical prefaces. Another of Isidore's works, *Etymologies*, was an encyclopedic introduction to the disciplines in which scholars should be trained. These disciplines included theology, grammar, mathematics, rhetoric, medicine, law, and music.[3] In his preface to the chapter on theology, Isidore listed all the biblical books. For the Old Testament, he provided both Hebrew and Greek titles for the Pentateuch.[4] Isidore's work and that of other Christian writers of the time described the

---

2 Bover y Oliver, "Vulgata en España," 11–40, 167–85.

3. Isidore is known as the patron saint of the internet because of his quest to collect and make available the widest possible collection of human knowledge.

4. Brehaut, *Encyclopedist of the Dark Ages*, 118–19.

political and religious currents that shaped early medieval Spanish identity, drawing on the cultures of both Germanic Visigoths and Hispano-Romans. In the midst of this cultural diversity, the Latin Vulgate remained dominant, and developments in that version can be observed in codices copied in Spain, some from before the Arab invasion and many from the century that followed.

The arrival of Arab armies in Iberia (711–713), and their conquest of much of the peninsula, brought major changes to the region. The conquerors brought with them a new culture, language, and faith, shaped by their own sacred text, the Qur'an. The Qur'an had from the beginning been accepted by Muslims as God's direct revelation to the prophet Muhammad. And by the time of the Spanish conquest, Muslim caliphs had settled on an agreed-upon text of their sacred book.[5] Many Spanish Jews welcomed the Arab forces, after suffering centuries of persecution by Christian rulers. Under those Visigoths, Spanish Jews had continued to study the Bible in Hebrew, thus orienting Spanish scholars to give Hebrew texts priority over Greek or Latin versions of the Old Testament. The introduction of a new sacred text, in the region now known as Al-Andalus, led to a complex multi-lingual environment for biblical study and translation.

For several centuries, Christians, Muslims, and Jews lived in uneasy but culturally rich interaction. Jews had always been a minority in the region, and neither Christian nor Muslim rulers dominated the entire peninsula. Some Spanish rulers began skirmishes which they called the Reconquista, attempting to push Muslims out of Spain. Nevertheless, while members of the three religious communities preferred to live within their own groups, much intercultural engagement was also in process. Several striking examples show the wide influence of this interaction, both in and beyond Spain: "Samuel ibn Nagrila, the great Jewish poet and vizier of the Taifa kingdom of Granada; Petrus Alfonsi, the converted Jew who introduced the English court of Henry I to the wonders of Arab science; Peter the Venerable, the abbot of Cluny who was responsible for overseeing the first Latin translation of the Qur'an; and Thomas Aquinas, whose controversial synthesis of Christian theology and Aristotelian philosophy

---

5. "Caliph" is the Arabic term for "successor," used in early Arab-Muslim history for leaders who succeeded Muhammed. According to tradition, the text of the Qur'an was standardized at the time of Muhammed's brother-in-law, Caliph Uthman (d. 656 CE).

was built of the foundations laid by Averroes [Ibn Rushd] and Maimonides [Moses ben Maimon]."[6]

Translation of the Bible into the medieval languages that would become Spanish began during this period. Under the reign of King Alfonso X (1221–1284), the city of Toledo, the capital of the kingdom of Castille, became a center of translation. Jewish intellectuals played active roles in the emergence of the Castilian language, and Christian translators drew on the Hebrew texts of the Bible for translating biblical portions into Castilian. Further north, Catalan speakers also began Bible translation.[7]

The role of rulers in promoting translation and intellectual inquiry was important during the Middle Ages. For example, a Castilian courtier in 1422 commissioned the rabbi Moshe Arragel to translate the entire Hebrew Bible into Castilian, together with notes and illustrations. Rabbi Moshe's correspondence with his Christian supervisors was reproduced in the first fifty pages of what became known as the *Biblia de Alba*. At first, the rabbi declined the job, noting that since his version might differ from translations from the Vulgate, it could offend Christian scholars. He also pointed out that because the Ten Commandments forbid the making of images, he could not provide illustrations. However, the rabbi later agreed to provide translation and commentary, and his notes showed his care to distinguish Jewish from Christian understandings. For example, on the word "apostle," Rabbi Moshe wrote: "For the Latins the word comes to mean the apostles that [preached] the faith of Jesus Christ. . . . And the Jews consider the apostles of God the holy fathers Abraham, Isaac, and Jacob, and the holy prophets."[8] As a representative of interfaith Bible scholarship, the *Biblia de Alba* was a rare survivor of what would soon take place, when, partly under pressure from Rome, Spanish rulers expelled the Jews from Spain.

In 1479, the marriage of Isabella, queen of Castile, and Ferdinand, king of Aragon, united large portions of Spain. Named "Catholic monarchs" by the pope, Isabella and Ferdinand led Reconquista armies that forced the last Arab rulers from Granada, the southernmost region of the Spanish peninsula. As the royal campaign succeeded, the Roman church was also setting up legal proceedings to root out religious dissenters. The full force of this Inquisition was exerted in Spain, including persecution of people and suppression of forbidden religious practices and books. Portions of Bibles

---

6. Wolf, "*Convivencia* in Medieval Spain."
7. Pérez Alonso, "Biblias Romanceadas," 398–99.
8. Ruiz and Nanko-Fernández, "Dialogues in the Margins," 42.

in the vernacular were burned. Jews who refused to convert were expelled from Spain. In response to this brutal mandate, some Jews led public lives as Christians, while continuing to practice their own faith in secret. Other Jews kept their Hebrew Bibles privately by copying texts in Castilian or other Romance languages using Hebrew characters.

During this period in medieval Spain, Jews and Muslims who converted to Christianity, usually under pressure, were called "new Christians," or *conversos*. Those who had been part of the Catholic faith for centuries were known as "old Christians." Prejudice against new Christians was intense, and the Inquisition dug even deeper, seeking those who continued private Jewish practice, also known as crypto-Jews.

Soon, though, the Inquisition confronted a new counter-challenge: some Spanish Christians were joining in theological debates going on elsewhere in Europe. In the early sixteenth century, Spanish monks, religious women, and laypersons met to read and discuss the Bible, and to consider reforms in church practices. They imagined a church that could still be "catholic," but not "Roman." The German theologian Martin Luther was becoming famous across Europe for his critique of the practice of the Roman church, and the inquisitors in Spain called their dissenters *luteranos*. However, many of the Spanish reformers were students of the Dutch philosopher Erasmus, who also criticized the Roman church while he remained within its community.

In 1516 in Switzerland, Erasmus had published an edition of the Greek New Testament, along with his own translation of the Greek into Latin. This work opened doors for readers, versed in the Latin Vulgate, to study and question some of the church's interpretations. Even before Erasmus's Greek edition, Spanish cardinal Ximenes de Cisneros had sponsored a similar project. His New Testament edition, prepared in part by *converso* scholars, offered parallel columns to present comparative readings between Hebrew, Greek, and Latin. Because Erasmus had gained first papal permission to publish, however, his edition was the one that quickly spread throughout Europe.

The impact of such new biblical readings led to further official restrictions. One imperial list of banned books, adopted by the Spanish Inquisition, declared: "Reading the Bible in our Spanish language or any other modern language is banned, in all or any part."[9] Under pressure, a group of reforming Spanish monks fled, some to Geneva and others to England. One

---

9. Serrano, *History of the Spanish Bible*, 53.

HOW DID THE BIBLE IN SPANISH DEVELOP?

of these fugitives, Casiodoro de Reina, in 1569 published a new translation of the Spanish Bible, a task that had taken him twelve years to complete. For the Old Testament, Reina used Hebrew manuscripts as well as a Hebrew Bible translated into Spanish by Jews who had fled to Italy, and the Greek New Testament edition prepared by Erasmus. For his own safety, Reina published the Bible in Geneva, because he knew that in 1562 he had been burned in effigy in the square of Seville. Reina's translation, revised and re-published in 1602 by his colleague Cipriano de Valera, used language characteristic of what literary scholars call golden-age Spanish writing. Its poetic flavor can be compared to that of the English King James Version, and may even have been used by the committee who translated the KJV.[10] The 1569 edition of this Bible was called the "Bear Bible" because its cover bore an etching of a bear reaching into a tree for honey. The inscription underneath, using the Hebrew of Isa 40, read: "The word of our God will stand forever."

> 7.1 *Casiodoro de Reina, in addition to his Spanish Bible translation, also wrote a confession of faith while in exile. Reina first published this confession of faith in Latin to introduce himself to exiled Reformed communities in England. In 1577, Reina published the same confession in Spanish, hoping to smuggle it back into Spain. Despite Reina's biblical scholarship, this confession does not include "discussion of biblical canon or of biblical revelation in general."*
>
> How the Prophetic work of the Christ is communicated to us. In this way we affirm that his Prophetic work is derived in us as we have said of his Kingship, and of the other roles of his Priesthood, by virtue of his teaching office to all those who truly belong to the Christian People, that are taught by God, and prophesy, that is to say, know how to declare the divine will in the world, which kind of doctrine and form of teaching we understand to belong to the New Testament, or better said, to be the practice of the same.[11]

The end of the Spanish Reconquista also opened the way for Isabella and Fernando to initiate Spanish military and merchant voyages westward across the Atlantic. The Spanish experience of religious warfare thus also became the foundation of the quest to extract gold and tobacco from the

---

10. Bonilla, "Cosas Olvidadas," 155–80.

11. Reina, *Declaration, or Confession of Faith,* 9.13. Capitalization in the text follows Spanish usage.

Americas, the expansion of the Atlantic trade in enslaved Africans, and the transmission of Catholic-Protestant hostility into the "new world." All of these forces shaped the Bible's translation and distribution throughout the Americas. So, while the long and rich story of the Bible in Spanish has continued in Europe, the rest of this chapter will focus on vignettes of the story as the Bible was introduced in the Americas.

Catholic clergy arrived in Mexico in the early 1500s, with a goal of teaching about and bringing to Christian faith Mexico's indigenous population. Yet by 1555, Spanish colonial officials had banned the training of local church leaders. Further, the Inquisition also came to Mexico, and Inquisition trial records revealed that studying the Bible was widespread among Indigenous, Lutheran, and crypto-Jewish peoples. Since in Spain Bibles in Spanish or Hebrew were already banned, authorities in Mexico began tracking down owners and sellers of those books. All boats arriving in Mexican ports were boarded before they docked, searched for banned books, and their crews interrogated. One question they were asked was whether they had "any forbidden books such as the Bible in any vernacular, or any other books of the Lutheran and calvinist sects and of other heretics, or any of those forbidden by the Holy office of the inquisition, or any others unregistered and concealed, or without license of the Holy office?"[12] This level of suspicion about biblical use also pushed Mexican leaders to seek to limit religious women who studied Scripture.

> 7.1 *Mexican nun Sor Juana Inés de la Cruz (1648–1695), a writer and composer, lived her whole life in Mexico. In this letter, Sor Juana responded to criticism from her bishop about her advanced theological studies and argued that she should be allowed to teach other nuns.*
>
> I obeyed [the order not to study] for the approximately three months that [the prelate] was in authority, and I did not take a book in hand. But not studying at all is not something that I can really do, nor could I do it then. Even though I did not study in books, I did study all the things that God has made, using them as letters, and the entire machine of the universe becoming a book. Nothing did I see without reflecting, nothing did I hear without thinking, and this even in the least and most material things, since there is no creature, no matter how low, in which one cannot acknowledge *me fecit Deus* (God made me). There is not one of them that does not overwhelm the mind, if it is properly considered.... For, why could not an elderly woman, learned in letters and of holy

---

12. Cuellar, "Forgotten Forebears," 126.

customs and conversation, take charge of maidens? But instead of that, these [maidens] are lost either by lack of teaching or by being taught by such dangerous means and by male teachers. It would be much less perilous for them to commit the indecency of sitting by an elder lady who would blush even when her own father looks into her face than for them to sit by a male stranger who deals with them with inappropriate familiarity and condescension.... But everyone knows that this is true and that it has to be allowed simply because there are no elder wise women. Therefore, it is a great evil that there are no such women. This should be a matter for consideration for those who, tied by *Mulieres in Ecclesia taceant* [let women be silent in church], condemn the notion that women might know and teach.[13]

Despite official sanctions, records from the colonial period in Mexico showed that distribution of the Bible continued apace. Inquisition trial accounts laid bare the efforts of some Mexican Jewish families to both maintain their access to the Bible and assure their children's education. The memoir of Luis de Carvajal offered a painful example of this practice. Carvajal told his inquisitors that he had purchased a Latin Vulgate Bible when he disembarked in Mexico from Spain in 1581. In addition to the Bible, his personal library included Christian devotional texts and "a small booklet of the Decalogue in Latin, which he sewed into the lining of his hat." At his trial, Carvajal admitted that he celebrated Passover with his family, reading the biblical texts from the Latin Vulgate and translating them into Spanish. Carvajal was imprisoned, but released in 1590, and assigned to teach Latin grammar and assist Mexican priests in their research.[14]

In 1642, Protestants arrived in Central America when the English claimed an island off Honduras to facilitate the slave trade. By the nineteenth century, however, some English Christians, especially among dissenting churches such as Methodists and Baptists, had joined the abolitionist movement. Their commitments intersected with the rising vision of Latin American leaders who sought independence from Spain. Liberation ideals, together with more free trade, led English settlers in Central America to begin distributing Bibles.[15]

13. González and González, *Nuestra Fe*, 69.
14. Cuellar, "Forgotten Forebears," 127, 130.
15. Prieto, "Historical Antecedents," 160–61.

Early in that century, Venezuelan patriot Simon Bolívar, who had met and was impressed by Joseph Lancaster, an English Quaker, adopted Lancaster's small-group approach to children's education. The Lancastrian method also impressed South American general José de San Martín, who in 1822 invited Scottish Baptist pastor James Thompson to set up this new educational program in Peru. Thompson, also a representative of the British and Foreign Bible Society, expanded his Bible distribution efforts into Mexico. Liberalizing education, promoting political independence, and studying the Bible went hand in hand. While many Catholic leaders resisted these activities, some priests were eager to cooperate with European Bible society distributors.[16]

During the nineteenth century these European Protestant Bible promoters distributed the Padre Scio Bible, a version from the Latin Vulgate published in Spain in the 1790s. In 1862, when the United Bible Societies published a revised translation based on the sixteenth-century reformers' work, they titled that version the Reina-Valera. The twentieth century brought further theological and theoretical changes that led to the preparation of new Spanish-language versions. Revised again in 1960, the Reina-Valera became the favored text for most Spanish-speaking Protestants/Evangelicals. In 1943, an encyclical from Pope Pius XII first permitted translations used by Catholics worldwide to be made using Hebrew and Greek editions of biblical texts, rather than the Latin Vulgate.

Also in the twentieth century, the translation theory advanced by linguist and philosopher Eugene Nida, called "dynamic equivalence," became widely influential. This theory argued that meaning in translation came from rendering ideas sense-for-sense, rather than narrowly word-for-word (see chapter 1). Throughout the Americas, tensions simmered between Protestant missionaries and Catholic leaders over the language choices and marketing plans of different Bible versions.[17] Yet it became the norm for translation teams to include both Protestant and Catholic scholars. In 1966, the United Bible Societies published the New Testament of the version *Dios Habla Hoy* (God Speaks Today), a popular language translation using dynamic equivalence methods. *Dios Habla Hoy* continues to be read across the ecclesial spectrum in Latin America.

The 1960 edition of the Reina-Valera also remains widely popular, in some settings taking on a status similar to that of the King James Version

---

16. Prieto, "Historical Antecedents," 177–78.
17. Voth, "Hacia una Ética de Liberación."

among many English-language readers.[18] In 1999, the International Bible Society published the *Nueva Versión Internacional* a Spanish-language translation using principles that had shaped the North American-based New International Version. Contributions to this version by prominent Ecuadorian theologian René Padilla and Mexican translator Alfredo Tepox enhanced the status of this version for some Spanish-language readers.

Political, economic, and theological developments have continued to shape how the Bible is read and translated among Spanish-speakers and readers in the Americas. Much of Central and South America suffered during the 1970s and 1980s under repressive military dictatorships. Courageous Catholic religious and lay teachers and many lay Christians participated in the base Christian community movement, where clergy and lay people were encouraged to read the Bible together as a message of liberation.

> 7.2 Ernesto Cardenal (1925–2020), a Nicaraguan Jesuit priest and liberation theologian, described a Bible study discussion among members of his congregation in the 1970s, reflecting on Matthew's Gospel account of the wise men.
>
> *Adán:* "It seems to me that when those wise men arrived they knew that the Messiah had been born and they thought Herod knew about it and that the Messiah was going to be a member of his family. If he was a king, it was natural that they should go to look for him in Herod's palace. But in that palace there was nothing but corruption and evil, and the Messiah couldn't be born there. He had to be born among the people, poor, in a stable. They learned a lesson there when they saw that the Messiah had not been born in a palace or in the home of some rich person, and that's why they had to go on looking for him somewhere else. The Gospel says later that when they left there they saw the star again. That means that when they reached Jerusalem the star wasn't guiding them. They'd lost it.
>
> *Félix:* "They were confused. And it seems to me that since they were foreigners they did not know the country very well, and they went to the capital, where the authorities were, to ask about the new leader."
>
> *Oscar:* "I figure that when Herod found out that that king had been born he was furious because he didn't want to stop being the ruler. He was as mad as hell. And he was already figuring out how to get rid of this one like he had got rid of so many already."

---

18. Bonilla, "Cosas Olvidadas," 166.

Pablo: "He must have felt hatred and envy. Because dictators always think they are gods. They think they're the only ones and they can't let anyone be above them."

Gloria: "And he was probably afraid, too. He had killed a lot of people not long before, and then some gentlemen arrive asking where's the new king, the liberator."

Félix: "He surely must have put all his police on the alert. I think that's what the Gospel means here: 'He was very troubled.'"[19]

By the mid-twentieth century, many Spanish-language Christian communities were also being energized by Pentecostal spirituality, leading to new interest in reading and contextualizing Scripture. This movement raised challenges in some settings by offering biblical readings promoting a prosperity gospel or supporting new forms of political repression. Yet Pentecostal influences were also liberating for many Spanish-language Christians.

> *7.2 Justo González, a Cuban-American theologian and church historian, recounted his experiences as a scholar trained in European methodology, as he came to a new appreciation of his identity as a Latino Christian.*
>
> [Reading in Spanish] takes up one of the fundamental symbols of who we are and raises it to the level of a hermeneutical method. Ada Maria Isasi-Diaz remembers her grandmother's reference to Spanish as "the language of the angels," and argues that "the Spanish language functions for Latinas not only as a means of communication but as a means of identification." . . . In fact, many of my Pentecostal friends were saying and doing much of what the Latin Mass and the Book of Prayer said and did, except that they were doing it "in Spanish"—in Spanish, not only in the sense that they did it in the vernacular, but also in the sense that they did it in ways that affirmed them and their culture. On the one hand we were taught to say: The Lord be with you/And with your Spirit. On the other, I heard: Buenas noches, hermanos, que el Señor les bendiga.[20]

---

19. González and González, *Nuestra Fe*, 182–85.
20. González, "Reading Ourselves in Spanish," 12–15.

Throughout the Americas, theologians such as González, as well as biblical scholars such as Jean-Pierre Ruiz and Esteban Voth, are recognized in the guild of international biblical scholars. Many Spanish-speaking churches in the Americas also promote the training of lay Bible teachers. Among Roman Catholics, different Spanish-language versions are used liturgically, for catechesis, and in personal devotion. The *Biblia de la Iglesia en América* version was initiated when the United States Conference of Catholic Bishops requested the Bishops Conference of Latin America for a Spanish-language Bible that they could use. The completed version began distribution in 2019.

Churches using Spanish as their language for worship and study are growing across the Americas, from south to north. It is clear that the story of the Bible in Spanish is far from over, and that the ways the Bible is read and lived out by Spanish-reading Christians will grow in exciting and often complex ways.

Chapter 8

How Did Medieval and Reforming Readers Interpret the Bible?

When Jesus began his ministry, he joined other Jews studying the Scriptures and seeking to carry them out in their own settings. Jesus's approach both reminded his hearers of what the Scriptures said and applied those Scriptures to himself. Sometimes he challenged earlier interpretations, as when he said: "You have heard that it was said . . . but I say unto you." He also underlined the continuity of his teaching with the Bible, when he said: "I have not come to destroy but to fulfill" (Matt 5). After his death and resurrection, Jesus's followers, both amazed and puzzled at their experiences, reviewed their Scriptures for clues to understand what had happened to Jesus and to them. In addition to their own study, they also debated with other Jews who read the Bible differently.

The history of biblical interpretation is long, complicated, and as rich a story as the one of how the Bible became a modern book. Since these two stories are interwoven, this chapter will observe how the two have shaped each other in one context, that of medieval Europe. Of course, biblical interpretation was much more ancient, beginning within the biblical library itself. For example, the Ten Words of Exodus were restated in Deuteronomy, the book whose Greek title means "Second Law." Those hearing what Moses pronounced on the verge of entering Canaan were reminded of their meeting with YHWH much earlier in the wilderness journey, and admonished to pass God's words on to the next generations. Readers also observe that the New Testament is a collection of ways Jesus and his followers used and interpreted Scripture. Mark's Gospel account of Jesus's crucifixion described him on the cross, quoting from Ps 22. John's Gospel pointed back to the first words of Genesis with its opening phrase, "In the beginning." The apostle Paul identified his interpretational education as a Pharisee (Phil 3:5). His emphasis on the resurrection of Jesus followed emerging Pharisee theology. And, like Jesus, he summed up God's law with words from Leviticus: "Love your neighbor as yourself" (Lev 19:18; Gal 5:14; Rom 13:9).

Within decades of Paul's life, descendants of the Pharisees, the rabbis, renewed their approaches to biblical commentary in the light of the destruction of the Jerusalem temple. Early rabbinic interpretation was called "midrash," from the Hebrew verb "to study." As noted earlier (chapter 6), rabbinic interpretation expressed with commentary was called the Mishnah. Over the centuries, this interpretational practice built a body of literature known as the Talmud. Among the characteristics of Talmudic interpretation was the method of recording lengthy threads of discussion, naming each rabbi who added to the commentary, as well as quoting earlier rabbis and additional biblical sayings.

> 8.1 *This excerpt from the Babylonian Talmud, which served as the basis for all further rabbinic law codes, commented on the importance of sabbath.*
>
> SAID the Holy One, blessed be He, to Moses: I have a precious gift in my treasure and its name is "Sabbath" and I wish to give it to Israel. Go and inform them of it. From this remark I infer, said Rabbi Simon ben Gamaliel, that if one gives a piece of bread to a child, he must inform the mother of it. How does one do it? He dabs him with oil and paints him with Kohl. But how about these days, when we are afraid of witchcraft? Rab Pupa says: One does the same. But it is not so. For Rabbi Hama ben Rabbi Hanina says: If one makes a gift to his neighbor one does not have to inform him for it was said: (*Exodus* xxxiv, 29) *Moses wist not that the skin of his face shone while he talked with him.* There is no contradiction here. In one instance, the fact will be evident in any case. In the other instance it may not be known. The Sabbath, too, was bound to be known. But its reward was not bound to be known.[1]

Pagan, Jews, and Christians were honing different interpretational methods in the intellectual schools of Alexandria in Egypt. These methods assumed

---

1. "Tractate Sabbath," in Auerbach, *Babylonian Talmud*, 58–59.

that texts needed to be studied to reveal philosophical and spiritual meanings within or beneath their words. The commentaries of Paul's contemporary, the first-century Jewish philosopher Philo, used allegory, for example when he identified the four rivers of Gen 2 as the virtues of prudence, graciousness, courage, and self-mastery.[2] Many gentile Christians also found this method useful, and it spread widely through the commentaries and homilies of Origen.

> 8.2 *Origen of Alexandria (ca. 189–ca. 257) studied with both pagan and Christian philosophers, as well as Jewish teachers. Origen often drew on allegory in his preaching. In this homily he introduced Joshua by pointing out that the names Jesus and Joshua are the same, and then drew on the New Testament to show how Joshua was Jesus.*
>
> Scripture says, "The Lord said to Jesus, the son of Nun, the assistant to Moses: 'Moses my servant is dead. Now, therefore, rising up, cross over this Jordan, you and all this people, into the land that I am giving you.'"
>
> Perhaps you seek to know in what way our Lord Jesus, the son of God, could also be the assistant of Moses. It is because "when the fullness of time had come, God sent his own son made of a woman, made under the Law." Through this, therefore, that he was "made under the Law," he became the "assistant of Moses."
>
> God tells them to cross over into the land, not the land Moses gave, but "that which I am giving to you." Therefore, you see that God gives the land to the people through Jesus after Moses was dead. What land? Doubtless, the land about which the Lord says, "Blessed are the meek, who will possess the land as their inheritance."[3]

Other early Christians interpreted Scripture more personally and directly. The third-century diary of the African matron Perpetua described what happened after she was imprisoned because she had become a Christian. Her prison visions "doubled" biblical visions, as she climbed a ladder "reaching all the way into the heavens" (Gen 28:12), "trod on the head" of a serpent/dragon (Gen 3:15), and encountered a white-haired man (Rev 1:14) surrounded by "thousands of people clad in white garments" (Rev

---

2. Philo, *Commentary on Genesis*, in *Works of Philo*, 2.
3. Origen, *Homilies on Joshua* 2.2.

7:9–14).⁴ Over the next centuries, pilgrims from around the Mediterranean traveled to the Holy Land to experiences the places and characters of the biblical story. One fourth-century monk, visiting the cave "where our Lord Himself shone forth from His chamber in the Virgin's womb," was moved to pledge that he would make another pilgrimage to Egypt.⁵ For many early pilgrims, Egypt was a holy place with monastics with biblical reputations. One collection of pilgrim stories described a monk who "looked like Abraham and had a beard like Aaron's," and others who could "raise the dead and walk on water just like Peter."⁶ According to one scholar, such personal biblical readings created the kind of story in which the pilgrim storyteller stood between the reader and the monk, and "collapsed the time" between the biblical characters and the experience of the readers.⁷

By the Middle Ages, intellectual theological centers of Europe had elaborated the approaches to biblical interpretation that grew from the work of earlier allegorists. The Doctrine of the Fourfold Sense articulated this process in a Latin rhyme as a memory aide for students:

> Lettera gesta docet,
> quid credas allegoria,
> Moralia quid agas,
> quo tendas, anagogia
>
> The letter teaches what was done,
> allegory what you are to believe,
> the moral sense what you are to do,
> the anagogical sense where you are to go.⁸

Although this multi-layered approach to Scripture was part of the formal training for Christian theologians, for many monastic communities the moral sense of Scripture took priority. Francis of Assisi (1181–1226) admonished those who joined his community: "The rule and life of the lesser brothers is this: To observe the holy gospel of our Lord Jesus Christ, living in obedience without anything of our own, and in chastity. . . . [After taking their vows] . . . let them go, sell all they have, and attempt to give it

---

4. Young, "Lady Advances," 263–82.
5. Cassian, *Conferences* 17.5.
6. Russell, *Lives of the Desert Fathers* 26, epil. 2.
7. Frank, *Memory of the Eyes*, 7.
8. Dawes, *Introduction to the Bible*, 44.

to the poor."[9] Yet other Christians interpreted Scripture in light of mystical experiences. Hildegard of Bingen (1098–1179), the German theologian and abbess, opened her theological tome *Scivias* by describing how her visions were illuminated by Scripture: "Heaven was opened and a fiery light of exceeding brilliance came and permeated my whole brain, and inflamed my whole heart and my whole breast, not like a burning but like a warming flame, as the sun warms anything its rays touch. And immediately I knew the meaning of the exposition of the scriptures, namely the Psalter, the gospel and the other catholic volumes of both the Old and the New Testaments."[10] In England, Julian of Norwich (d. after 1416) recounted how God was revealed as she was healed from serious illness. Her imagery wove together the Ephesians language of the church as the body of Christ and John's description of Jesus's crucifixion: "The whole Body of Holy Church was never broken, nor never shall be, without end. And therefore a sure thing it is, a good and a gracious, to will meekly and mightily to be fastened and oned to our Mother, Holy Church, that is Christ Jesus. For the food of mercy that is His dearworthy blood and precious water is plenteous to make us fair and clean."[11]

During the fourteenth century, much of the world was shaken by the "Great Death," a pandemic that killed millions of people. Also, violent religious-themed crusades to the Holy Land, battles between rival popes, the disintegration of feudal economic systems, and the growth of cities as commercial centers reshaped life for many Europeans. In the same period, European intellectuals had discovered the works of Muslim philosophers and Eastern Christian scholars who came to the West after Constantinople fell to Turkish forces in 1453. All these thinkers expanded theories of interpretation. At the same time, most Christians could read little if at all, had no access to the Bible outside the church, and could no longer comprehend the Latin Vulgate. What most people knew of the Bible came through feast day celebrations, paintings, icons, sculptures, and popular plays that retold biblical stories.

In western Europe society had for centuries been organized, often not peacefully, in a combined religious and political system known as Christendom. Politically, the structure that emerged under Charlemagne (747–814) and those who succeeded him became known as the Holy Roman Empire.

---

9. Francis of Assisi, *Rule* 1–2.
10. Børresen and Valerio, *High Middle Ages*, 206.
11. Julian of Norwich, *Showings*, Revelation 14, ch. 61.

Its emperors navigated their realm in tense interaction with the Roman Catholic Church. While some princes and nobles were preoccupied with pushing back Arab Muslim rulers from their borders in Spain and repulsing Turkish Muslim armies to the east, European national identities also began to emerge. With those identities, languages descended from or different from Latin became widely used. The crusades into the Middle East, ironically, also renewed curiosity among Europeans about what the Bible said about Jesus, in the languages they understood.

During these centuries, portions of vernacular Bibles were circulating in Poland, Italy, Belgium, the Netherlands, and Germany, used by clergy, literate lay religious communities, nobles and wealthy merchants. "Censorship measures, however, existed in England and Spain, where the official Church had to deal with what it considered erroneous 'Bible-based' faith-systems."[12] By the sixteenth century, two Catholic scholar-theologians loudly advocated for Bibles that people could understand. As we saw in chapter 6, the arguments of Dutch humanist Desiderius Erasmus and German professor Martin Luther influenced thinkers throughout Europe. Erasmus, known for satirizing his own Roman Catholic Church, wrote in the introduction to his edition of the Greek New Testament: "I would have the weakest woman read the Gospels and Epistles of St. Paul.... I would have those words translated into all languages, so that not only Scots and Irishmen, but Turks and Saracens might read them. I long for the plowboy to sing them to himself as he follows the plow, the weaver to hum them to the tune of his shuttle, the traveler to beguile with them the dullness of his journey."[13]

Although other German-language Bibles had been prepared, Martin Luther undertook a new translation in 1521 while hiding from an imperial arrest order under the protection of a German prince. Rather than depending on the Latin Vulgate for his translation, Luther used the Greek New Testament text edited by Erasmus, and the Hebrew text of the Old Testament. Luther also publicly agitated for an end to the Latin mass, so that worship experiences would make sense to ordinary Germans. He was known for walking into nearby market towns to listen to ordinary people so that his translation would be able to use expressions that they recognized.

In the midst of this ferment, another theological debate arose: how to practice baptism as the rite of entry into the Christian community. Since

---

12 François, "Vernacular Bible Reading," 23.

13. Durant, *Reformation*, 285.

the earliest days of the Jesus movement, baptism had been the central event marking entry into the Christian community. Matthew's Gospel recorded Jesus commanding his followers to make disciples among all the nations of the world, "baptizing them in the name of the Father and of the Son and of the Holy Spirit" (Matt 28:19). Baptism in Christian communities included a water ritual of pouring or sprinkling on the candidate or immersing the candidate in a body of water. These different practices came from ways that Christians read different New Testament stories about baptism.

For centuries, churches in Africa and Central Asia as well as Europe had baptized infants born into Christian families. Baptism was understood as the way that God cleansed the original sin into which all humans were born. In some political and cultural settings, baptism was also a way to record births and keep church and citizenship records. Despite the many conflicts and schisms that troubled Christians throughout Europe and the Middle East during the Middle Ages, most Christians agreed that there should be only *one* church. Since baptism was how people were registered as members of the church, practices that muddied the waters were suspect if not dangerous.

Thus, when some Christians began to argue that being baptized should reflect a conscious adult choice to follow Jesus Christ and a commitment to living in Christlike ways, their views were seen by the authorities as a threat. These people, shaped by an approach to the Bible that called hearers to do what the text simply demanded, studied baptism accounts in Acts—at Pentecost, for the Ethiopian official, and for Saul/Paul. They read that all of these people were baptized after choosing to become followers of Jesus. Such a decision, they argued, not the wishes of church authorities or family, should determine when someone was baptized. While many authorities viewed rebaptism as an act of defiance, for those who became known as Anabaptists, or re-baptizers, adult baptism was not rebaptism, but the first true baptism. Opponents of this interpretation used the term "Anabaptist" as an insult, pointing to another story in Acts, when Paul and Silas baptized the entire household of their jailor. Everyone continued to see baptism as essential to Christian identity. The debate circled around when it should happen and who should choose when baptism took place.

After joining other reformers in debates about baptism, in 1525 a group of Swiss Christians in Zurich took the radical step of baptizing one another. This practice spread as traveling preachers such as Melchior Hoffman, originally among the followers of Luther, were rebaptized. In one dramatic moment in 1530, Melchior re-baptized more than three hundred people in a church in the Netherlands.[14]

Disagreements over baptism were part of a much broader movement of dissent among Christians in late medieval Europe. The ways that different groups of believers framed their arguments and their practices also differed. In the sixteenth century, Martin Luther was also well known for popularizing and proclaiming *sola Scriptura*, Scripture alone, as a principle of faith. However, Luther, a doctor of biblical theology, came from a different intellectual and social class than other reformers, including early Anabaptists, many of whom were peasants or tradespeople. While Anabaptists learned much from Luther and other reformers, they quickly differed in their insistence that the Bible could be read, understood, and applied by ordinary people.

Menno Simons, a Dutch priest who left his parish in 1536 and was rebaptized at about that time, wrote an account of how he decided to quit his ecclesial post. This memoir described Menno for the first time turning to the Bible, about which he had known very little, when he learned of the persecution of Anabaptists. As he read the Bible, Menno discovered that what it taught was clear and accessible to ordinary Christians.

> 8.3 *After he left the priesthood, Menno (1496–1561) spent decades as an itinerant pastor among scattered Anabaptist communities in northern Europe. Menno also wrote biblical and theological treatises, defenses of his new faith to the authorities, and letters to his churches. This text comes from his "Foundations of Christian Doctrine."*
>
> You say, we are inexpert, unlearned, and know not the Scriptures. I reply: The Word is plain and needs no interpretation: namely, Thou shalt love the Lord thy God with all thy heart, and with all thy soul, and with all thy strength, and thy neighbor as thyself. Mt 22:37, 39. Again, You shall give bread to the hungry and entertain the needy. Is 58:7. If you live according to the flesh you shall die, for to be carnally minded is death. The avaricious, drunkards, and the proud shall not inherit the kingdom of God. God will condemn adulterers and fornicators. Rom 8; 1 Cor. 6 and many like passages. All who do not understand such passages are more like irrational creatures than men, more like clods than Christians.[15]

14 See the survey of sixteenth-century Anabaptist history in Snyder, *Anabaptist History and Theology*.

15. Menno Simons, *Complete Writings*, 214.

From Word to Book

Sixteenth-century Anabaptists continued to read the Bible as a guide to practical living. In Switzerland, a group of Anabaptists hashed out answers to specific questions on which they differed from other Christians, whom they labeled "false brethren."

> 8.4 *In 1527, a gathering of Anabaptists worked out a set of shared guidelines for faithful living, known as the Schleitheim Confession. The resulting statement responded to seven questions: baptism, ban (excommunication), the breaking of bread, separation from abomination (relationship with other Christians), shepherds in the congregation (pastors), the sword, and the oath. The group's conclusion about baptism was based on "the writings of the apostles."*
>
> Baptism should be given to all those who have been taught repentance and the changing of life and who truly believe that their sins are taken away by Christ, and to all those who desire to walk in the resurrection of Jesus Christ and be buried with Him in death, so that they might rise with Him; to all those who with such an understanding themselves desire and request it from us with this understanding; given this [understanding] all infant baptism is excluded, the worst and first abomination of the pope. For this you have the foundation and the testimony of Scripture and the practice of the apostles.[16]

In the wake of the conflicts that grew from the Reformation, Protestant publishers began to collect and circulate stories of persecution of believers. The *Martyrs Mirror*, first published in Holland in 1660, opened with stories of martyrs from the beginning of the Christian movement. Its goal, however, was to represent the faithful witness of the Anabaptist martyrs of the editor's own century, who had suffered under both Protestant and Catholic rulers. In the *Martyrs Mirror*, accounts about Anabaptists, which cover more than half of the text's eleven-hundred pages, emphasized that their opponents were surprised by the Anabaptists' knowledge of the Scriptures. Hadewijk, a Dutch Anabaptist, escaped from her pursuers and was hidden in an attic by a "half-wit" man. When he made sexual advances to her, Hadewijk told him to stop, arguing that since she was married, sexual activity would make them both adulterers. "The jade is too wise in the

---

16. "Schleitheim Confession," author's translation based on text in Baecher, 46–47.

Scriptures," the man said; "I have no chance with her," and helped her to flee to safety.[17]

Another account described the interrogation of Claesken, using letters she wrote in 1559 to her community, who gave her answer when she was interrogated about not having her children baptized: "I cannot find it in the Scriptures, that this ought to be." At the tribunal before her execution, she insisted that an Anabaptist "brother had proved everything so clearly to him with the Scriptures that [the judge] could not say a single word against it." Finally, she asked the interrogator how her husband, who was also imprisoned, had responded to questioning. "He replied, 'Your husband also persists in his views.' I said: 'What will you do with my poor husband, who cannot read a word?' He replied: 'Your damnation will be greater than that of your husband, because you can read, and have seduced him.'"[18]

Snyder demonstrated that the extensive Anabaptist knowledge of Scripture was made possible by collections of texts on themes that were deemed central to faith, such as repentance, faith, and baptism. In that way, even those who could not read could hear and memorize the key verses that they then quoted under examination.[19] Murray, from his survey of early Anabaptist writings, distilled six interpretational keys that appeared in their work. First, as Menno had argued, Scripture is self-interpreting; all believers were capable of reading the Bible for themselves. But second, a critical move that shaped how the first key was effective, Anabaptists read the Bible Christocentrically. For them, Scripture pointed to Jesus, and discerning the meaning of Jesus's words and life called for the Holy Spirit's aid as interpreter.

Third, Anabaptists recognized that reading the Old Testament could pose difficulties for Christians. Thus, they tended to read the two Testaments at different levels, at times turning to spiritual interpretations of difficult passages. Yet they did not abandon the Old Testament, always seeking its Christocentric focus. Fourth, Anabaptists believed that Christians could hear God's voice expressed both inwardly and within the community, through the work of the Holy Spirit. They insisted that the Spirit's inspiration had to agree with the teachings of Jesus and that the Spirit's work would bring believers to agreement. Fifth, Anabaptists read the Bible together. They insisted that the best interpretation would be done in gathered

17. Bragt, *Martyrs Mirror*, 616. See also Heisey, "Women."
18. Bragt, *Martyrs Mirror*, 547.
19. Snyder, *Following in the Footsteps*, 117–22.

bodies of believers, not at the university or solely by individuals. And sixth, they followed a "hermeneutic of obedience." At its most basic, this approach meant that to truly understand the Bible, Christians needed to do what it said. Within this framework they insisted on avoiding interpretations that led to ethically questionable actions.[20]

Centuries of ecclesial, historical, and social changes have continued to challenge and expand ways that Bible readers have interpreted the text. Western models and questions have encountered the power of texts and practices from other faith traditions. The worldwide expansion of the Christian movement into many cultures and languages, while part of the Christian story from the early centuries of the movement, has from the twentieth century exploded ways of reading and knowing. In many settings, the separatist stance that shaped some Christian groups, including Anabaptists, has given way to an interest in learning and borrowing from a range of cultures and interpretational traditions. Before returning to a discussion of what is happening among biblical readers in the twenty-first century, we must consider several examples of how modern exploration and discovery had an impact on ways of understanding the Bible. Thus our next question will be to explore some scientific and historical discoveries and debates that have challenged traditional understandings about the Bible.

---

20. Murray, *Biblical Interpretation*, 206–16.

Chapter 9

How Have Modern Discoveries Impacted Understandings of the Bible?

Much of the story we have considered so far draws on modern research about historically ancient and culturally distant times. Until the twentieth century, Europeans and North Americans had the greatest access to the Bible in print; thus, many of the questions in this chapter arose first in those regions. Nevertheless, new insights about the Bible, based on modern discoveries, have also interested and challenged readers around the world. Researchers in disciplines from archaeology to paleontology, from astronomy to physics, from evolutionary biology to genetics, and from geology to environmental science have dramatically shaped conversations about the Bible.

Finding additional manuscripts of any ancient text rouses critical questions for scholars. In fact, text studies have been important in literature even for more recent works. Many theater lovers, for example, do not know that neither actors nor editors have anything from Shakespeare's own hand. Further, his most well-known plays are published in more than one printed edition. Editors have to choose between editions, for example, one of which names the mischievous *Midsummer Night's Dream* character "Puck" and another "Robin Goodfellow."[1]

Since such questions can confront people reading or performing a sixteenth-century English play, it is clear that editors of the Bible have an even more difficult task. As we have seen, biblical texts were written down

---

1. Shakespeare & Beyond, "Barbara Mowat on Editing Shakespeare."

and copied over centuries, in both ancient Hebrew and Koine Greek, the trade language of the Greco-Roman world. Often without named authors, ancient biblical manuscripts are available in a dizzying variety of fragments and complete texts. For the New Testament, thousands of ancient Greek manuscripts have been catalogued.[2]

Ancient readers and hearers recognized that their cherished stories often appeared in more than one written form. In the first century, Josephus retold many of the stories that also appear in the Christian Old Testament; at times his versions, written in Greek, clarify events that are obscure in Hebrew manuscripts. For example, see the note before 1 Sam 11, in the NRSV. In Egypt, Origen recognized the significance of comparing biblical manuscripts, so he edited a six-column edition of biblical texts comparing two Hebrew texts and four different Greek translations of the Bible. To clarify these comparisons, Origen developed a symbol system that identified specific points where the texts differed from each other. As a preacher, Origen also noted textual differences, for example when he referred to a text in Matthew's Gospel that named Isaiah as the author of a psalm, rather than Asaph as the name appeared in the Old Testament texts.[3]

Ancient readers also discussed the meaning of difficult words in scriptural accounts. On a puzzling geographical reference, Origen argued that when John's Gospel (1:28) described where John the Baptist was baptizing, the text named the wrong location. He further declared that he knew where Bethany was, because he had actually visited there.[4] Adding to the importance of studying manuscript evidence, in recent years scholars have recognized that Jesus's words in the New Testament are recorded in Greek. Yet they know, given his Galilean childhood, that Jesus probably spoke Aramaic, a sister language to Hebrew. The prayer that Jesus taught his disciples, quoted in Matthew and Luke, included a puzzling Greek word to describe the bread that people requested. While the word for "bread" is clear, the adjective describing it is not. Jerome, the fourth-century Bible translator, used three different Latin words in an effort to understand the biblical Greek term.[5] Some linguists have tried to back-translate to determine what Jesus meant when he taught this request, in Aramaic.[6]

2. Center for the Study of New Testament Manuscripts, "Manuscripts 101."
3. Mitchell, "Origen and the Text-Critical Dilemma," 70.
4. Dorfbauer, "Bethania, Bethara, or Bethabara."
5. Burton, *Abba Isn't Daddy*, 119.
6. Shapira, "Our Daily Bread Is at Risk," 1097–101.

HOW HAVE MODERN DISCOVERIES IMPACTED UNDERSTANDINGS

More textual discoveries were uncovered in late medieval Europe. Despite centuries of preeminence for the Latin Vulgate as the authoritative text, in the fifteenth and sixteenth centuries, scholars developed new interest in the Greek New Testament. This interest, bolstered by the invention of the printing press and access to more Greek manuscripts, aroused hope for a published Greek New Testament for publication. One such edition was printed in Spain in 1514, but the first published version came out in 1516. The Dutch philosopher Erasmus, editor of this edition, defended his work in the dedication to Pope Leo: "I perceived that that teaching which is our salvation was to be had in a much purer and more lively form if sought at the fountain-head and drawn from the actual sources than from pools and runnels. And so I have revised the whole New Testament (as they call it) against the standard of the Greek original."[7]

In the 1630s, publishers used the Latin term *textus receptus* in an advertising blurb to identify the "received text" of the Greek New Testament used in their Bible. It is common to say that the 1611 King James Bible was based on the Textus Receptus, but in fact the King James translators used two different Greek editions from Erasmus. For the New Testament, those translators also chose sixty-seven text variants that they found in sources other than the two Erasmian editions. And scholars continued to revise editions of the Textus Receptus until 1881.[8]

For the Old Testament, scholars using the well-established medieval Masoretic Text (MT) pointed back to the work of Jerome, the model for biblical translators. Already in the fourth century, Jerome had preferred Hebrew to Greek as the foundation for his Latin Old Testament version. Until the discovery of biblical manuscripts among the Dead Sea Scrolls, the MT continued to be the basis for new versions. Although translators also had copies of ancient Greek translations from Hebrew, for centuries they considered those manuscripts inferior when compared with the Masoretic Text. Now textual studies of the Hebrew Bible must consider Qumran and other manuscripts that are more than eight hundred years older. A new critical edition of the Hebrew Bible is now being prepared for translators, taking into account recent manuscript evidence.[9]

Modern translations of the New Testament are based on what editors call an "eclectic text," that is, a Greek edition that brings together what

---

7. Combs, "Erasmus and the Textus Receptus," 44.
8. Ward, "Which Textus Receptus?," 53.
9. Society of Biblical Literature, "Hebrew Bible."

scholars consider the best readings. Although the fourth-century Codex Sinaiticus, one of the earliest complete New Testaments, was translated into English in 1866, discovery of even older papyri fragments pushed British scholars Wescott and Hort to prepare a new eclectic Greek edition, published in 1881.[10] Their edition became the basis for the United Bible Societies/Nestlé-Aland Greek editions widely used by translators today. However, some Bible versions continue to be based on the 1881 edition of the Textus Receptus. Most contemporary Bible versions include an introduction identifying which Greek edition(s) they used, as well as notes explaining their choices of particular readings. Thus everyday readers who prefer the New King James, the New International, the New Revised Standard, or the Common English versions, while most are unaware of this, are also choosing different eclectic editions of the Greek New Testament.

Many Bibles today offer footnotes to provide readers with information about some significant textual choices. A footnote might admit that the meaning of a word is obscure (Ps 2:11–12) or point out the use of different verbs used in different manuscripts (Mark 15:12). Editorial introductions usually explain how such matters have been handled. Careful scholarly work continues to explore ranges of meaning in both great and small differences among ancient manuscripts. Consider the following examples:

> 9.1 *The texts of Jeremiah*: In most English-language Bibles, Jeremiah has fifty-two chapters. The Septuagint (LXX) version of Jeremiah is about 2700 words shorter than the Masoretic Text (MT), and some of its prophetic oracles are placed in different order than in the MT. Some Christians read from translations of the LXX, but most have preferred versions from the Hebrew text. Recent studies, including texts of Jeremiah found at Qumran, show that the Greek versions were following a different Hebrew tradition rather than translating one tradition poorly. Because Jeremiah was describing the events surrounding the final Babylonian destruction of Jerusalem and the exile of many of its inhabitants, likely those who preserved Jeremiah's oracles had access to different parts of the story. Jeremiah himself ended up as a refugee in Egypt (see Jer 43), while over four thousand Judeans were taken captive to Babylon (Jer 52).[11]
>
> 9.2 *Angels sing to shepherds*: Many Christmas carols repeat the angels' song to the shepherds: "Peace on earth, good will to men/

---

10. Metzger and Ehrman, *Text of the New Testament*, 129.
11. Heater, "Once More, Jeremiah 10:4–10," 301–11.

HOW HAVE MODERN DISCOVERIES IMPACTED UNDERSTANDINGS

all." Most recent translations of Luke 2:14, in English and other languages, see this footnoted alternative: "Peace on earth, good will to those whom God favors." The first message is beloved as a promise that God's blessing is for the whole world; the second seems to limit peace to God's chosen people. Why? The difference in Greek is the spelling of one word, the word for "favor/good will." And the spelling difference in Greek is one letter, the word *eudokia* with or without an "s" at the end. Both word spellings are found in the most ancient manuscripts of Luke. It is likely that scribes either heard the text wrong or made a small mistake in copying. In this case, study of Qumran texts aided scholars in choosing "those whom God favors." Describing God's people as "people of favor" is frequently attested in Qumran manuscripts. Elsewhere, Luke's gospel consistently underlines that God's plan includes all people, but in this specific song, Luke seems to be quoting ancient Hebrew hymns.[12]

For New Testament text study, scholars have tried to trace the evolution of different texts of the Greek New Testament, copied over time, and the versions made from those manuscripts (see appendix C). For both Greek and Hebrew, textual decisions are based on guidelines elaborated by scholars, which include detecting ancient scribal errors, as well as those scribes' corrections or marginal notes; comparing other uses of the same word or phrase within one manuscript, and comparing the earliest biblical translations into Latin, Syriac, or Coptic. Although not all scholars agree, most work with the principle that shorter texts are usually closer to the earliest wording, since it would be normal for scribes to add words to assure that they were not missing anything important. For some scholars, the complexity of textual studies has given rise to skepticism about ancient scribal practices and arguments that some ancient biblical manuscripts are corrupt. Other scholars affirm that careful textual analysis is necessary to enrich biblical readings.

While detailed textual study of biblical manuscripts continues, modern textual discoveries are far from the only phenomena that have challenged how contemporary faith communities read the Bible. European colonial expansion and military conquest often paved the way for such challenges. European monarchs, competing on the seas, sent their sailors to search for new territories to exploit. Markets for enslaved persons and gold radically reshaped

---

12. Wolters, "Anthrōpoi Eudokias (Luke 2:14)," 291–92.

economic life. Adventurers uncovered artifacts from lands where the Bible had emerged. Deciphering ancient cuneiform tablets in Mesopotamia and hieroglyphic monuments in Egypt allowed biblical stories to be compared to texts from neighboring ancient cultures. Decades of religious wars in Europe led some to become cynical about church authority and its theological claims. Nevertheless, Christian clergy and Jewish rabbinic scholars remained at the center of biblical research, continually seeking to integrate what they learned with the continuing importance of the Scripture in their communities.

One important question raised by both historians and philosophers had to do with what could be known about the Bible's human authors. In medieval European universities, authors and the theories named after them were closely linked, whether theologians such as Augustine or Aquinas, or classical writers such as Aristotle or Plutarch. From well before New Testament times, Jews had referenced Moses as the author of the Torah. And as we saw in chapter 5, New Testament writers used Scripture with the formula "it is written," and cited their sources as "Moses and the prophets." While naming those human authors, New Testament writers understood God as the source of Scripture, even if behind the text, as when Stephen told his judges that the law came through the dictation of angels (Acts 7:53).

The medieval Jewish theologian Maimonides/Ben Maimon insisted that the Torah, given to Moses at Mount Sinai, was "from heaven." Yet observations of the natural world led other medieval theologians to describe God's revelation as two-fold: in the "book of nature" and the "book of Scripture."[13] In the sixteenth century, John Calvin declared that humans needed the "spectacles" of Scripture to read "the book of nature" accurately.[14] Thus, theologians acknowledged that God's revelation came in different forms, and often chose metaphorical language to draw a richer frame around perspectives on the authorship of Scripture.

The concept of human authorship of written texts remained important, however. In Greco-Roman thought, the term "author" had had a wide range of meaning: "creator, maker, author, inventor, producer, father, founder, teacher, composer." In Europe, named authors, even from antiquity, were identified with their published works.[15] In the seventeenth century, Jewish philosopher Spinoza wondered about Mosaic authorship of the Torah as he observed both its diverse genres and philosophical approaches. Although

---

13. Cooperrider, *Speak with the Earth*, 1–12.
14. Calvin, *Institutes* I.vi.1.
15. Bauerschmidt, "God as Author," 576.

Spinoza's questions led to his expulsion from an Amsterdam synagogue, these questions were not silenced. Further, in the wake of sixteenth-century Protestant claims that Scripture alone was necessary for faith, Roman Catholic theologians replied that church tradition was also necessary for correct interpretation. Since both rabbinic and ecclesial traditions almost always cited known authors, however, this insistence complicated the understanding of biblical authorship. Rather than settling these disputes, at least among Christians, such citations complicated thinking about who really assured biblical authority.[16]

In the eighteenth century, as noted in chapter 2, German scholars tried to uncover something of the authors who had shaped the sources behind the Hebrew Bible's text. The ancient identities of those earliest authors, scholars proposed, were revealed by different language styles, places where biblical stories seemed to repeat themselves, and different vocabulary for God. This source criticism often relegated Mosaic authorship into the background, as scholars focused attention on what might have come first. Careful reading of the prophets elicited similar observations. For example, the first part of the book attributed to the prophet Isaiah recounted events from the time of Judah's monarchs in the seventh century BCE. Yet later in the book, the prophetic word looked forward to the conquests of the Persian king Cyrus, who lived two hundred years later. And Daniel, according to the book bearing his name, lived during Babylonian captivity, yet the work also described Persian and Greek rulers from centuries later.

Among New Testament writings, scholars accepted the apostle Paul as a known historical author in the first-century Jesus-believing community. Paul's location in the historical record could be linked by inscriptions found by archeologists, specifically of Gallio, a Roman governor, and Erastus, city treasurer of Corinth (Rom 16:23; Acts 18:12–17, 19:22). The collected writings of Paul provided a clear sense of this author's language choices and rhetorical style; observations of Paul's vocabulary and rhetoric made it possible to evaluate all thirteen letters that bore his name. Careful readers observed that 1–2 Timothy and Titus, known as the Pastoral Letters, used more than three hundred words not found in Paul's other letters.

Equally noteworthy, while Jesus was the center of the entire biblical story for Christians, neither the New Testament writers nor other sources claimed that he had written anything. For early Christians, the authority of the gospel was tied to the belief that Jesus's words had been handed down

---

16. Barton, *History of the Bible*, 418.

in an unbroken chain of transmission from his first apostles. As noted in chapter 5, sayings of Jesus were remembered from outside the biblical textual record. Apostolicity as a principle, however, that is linking of text with Jesus's first disciples and their immediate descendants, became more important than any modern concept of authorship.

In recent discourse, although scholars continue to probe authorship questions, church leaders across the spectrum of institutional and theological perspectives have focused rather on articulating what it means to claim that God is the author of Scripture, while affirming the active role of human writers. Southern Baptists (2000) assert that: "The Holy Bible was written by men divinely inspired.... It has God for its author." The Roman Catholic catechism (1992) states: "God inspired the human authors of the sacred books." The Mennonite Confession of Faith (1995) declares: "Through the Holy Spirit, God moved human witnesses to write what is needed for salvation." Among Jews, both Orthodox and Conservative communities assert Maimonides's principle about the divine origin of the Torah, while the Reformed Jewish movement, emerging in nineteenth-century Europe, declares that: "Reform Judaism... views both the Oral and Written laws as a product of human hands."[17]

In recent centuries, rather than studying who first wrote about Jesus or what theologians have claimed about him, many people have become more interested into what can be known about the Jesus in his own first-century historical context. Based on Gospel portraits, Jesus grew up in Galilee (Matt 2:23), was a skilled artisan (Mark 6:3), and could read (Luke 4:16). All of the biblical records agree that Jesus was a teacher and a healer, and that he was arrested and crucified under the Roman governor Pilate. According to Roman records, Pilate, an obscure Roman politician, governed Judea from 26–36 CE. During the century when New Testament writers were recording these details, Jewish historian Josephus also mentioned Jesus twice. First, Josephus reported that Pilate ordered Jesus's crucifixion; his second mention was of James, a leader of the Jerusalem community, as "the brother of Jesus, who was called Christ."[18]

The title *christos* which both the apostle Paul and Josephus used for Jesus was the Greek translation of the Hebrew "messiah." This Christ title began to appear in other sources within the next century. Two Roman writers used Latin words, likely based on *christos*, to refer to groups whose

---

17. "Reform Judaism," §2.
18. Josephus, *Antiquities*, in *Flavius Josephus*, 20.9.1.

practices aroused imperial suspicion. One, a letter from a governor in Asia Minor to the emperor, described two women who were part of a small group who sang hymns "to Christ as a god."[19] The other, by a biographer of twelve Roman emperors, described the rulers' persecution and suppression of a group called "Christians."[20] Yet neither of these texts made any connections between this group and a historical person named Jesus.

The apostle Paul, the theologian who as far as we know first quoted or alluded to sayings from Jesus, called them "the word of the Lord" (e.g., 1 Thess 4:13). As we saw in chapter 5, the focus of Paul's letters was primarily on his theology of Jesus's crucifixion and resurrection, the two events that he believed demonstrated Jesus's identity as the Christ. During the following centuries, stories of Jesus's death and resurrection were a central and accepted focus of the Christian message. For centuries, both in ancient and medieval churches, it was the puzzle of how, and to what extent, Jesus was divine, rather than his historical reality, that called forth sometimes violent debate. Still, the most ancient statements of faith carefully rooted Jesus in his own time with two human names: Mary, who gave birth to him, and Pilate, who crucified him.

Much later, Europeans influenced by new historical information about the first-century settings of the Gospels began to write their own biographies of Jesus. Colonial exploration had expanded European awareness of human diversity and ancient history, but had also tempted them to assume their own cultural superiority. Descriptions of Jesus often resembled the people and places who wrote them.

> 9.3 *Ernst Renan (1823–1892) was a French philosopher who considered the relationship of faith to science. He participated on several research trips to Lebanon and Palestine in the early 1860s, and his* Life of Jesus, *published in 1863, revealed insights gleaned from those visits. Although condemned by church leaders, his writing was widely popular.*
>
> This happy and satisfying Galilean life . . . was spiritualized through ethereal dreams, with a kind of poetic mysticism that intermingled heaven and earth. Leave behind the severe John the Baptist in his Judean desert, thundering ceaselessly, eating grasshoppers and accompanied by jackals. Why should the friends of the bridegroom fast while the bridegroom is with them? Joy will

---

19. Pliny the Younger, "Letter 10 to Trajan," in *Complete Letters*, 278–79.
20. Suetonius, *Lives of the Twelve Caesars* 5.25.4, 6.16.

be part of the reign of God. Is God's reign not the daughter of the humble in heart, the people of good will?

Jesus never married. All his power of love directed itself toward what he thought of as his heavenly vocation. The extremely delicate feeling toward women that we can observe was never separated from his exclusive devotion to his calling. Like Francis of Assisi [who had his Saint Clare] he treated as sisters the women who were passionate about the same task as he.... But doubtless he was more beloved than loving. As often happens in elevated natures, his tenderness of heart was transformed in him into an infinite sweetness, a vague poetry, a universal charm.[21]

Taking a different point of view, in 1910 humanitarian doctor and New Testament scholar Albert Schweitzer published *The Quest for the Historical Jesus*. Schweitzer argued that Jesus was an apocalyptic prophet. However, said Schweitzer, when the dramatic inbreaking of God's reign Jesus had promised did not take place, his followers began revising their understanding of Jesus, leading to the early church struggles to nail down statements of belief about Jesus's divinity.

In the twentieth century, debates flourished about the relationship between "the Jesus of history" and the "Christ of faith." In the aftermath of the genocide of Jews before and during World War II, European and North American readers were forced to admit how Christian interpretations of Scripture had both laid a foundation for and sustained anti-Judaism. New research emphasized ways that the New Testament affirmed the Jewishness of Jesus. Careful reading of how first-century Jews used terms such as "son of God" and "Messiah" gave new perspectives into the Gospels' descriptions of Jesus. Scholars also challenged the traditional Christian story depicting a sharp and early split between Jews and Christians.[22]

In 1985 a group of scholars formed the Jesus Seminar, with the mission to publicize debates on different scholarly claims about the first-century Jewish man named Jesus. Among their assumptions was that Schweitzer's idea of Jesus as an apocalyptic prophet was incorrect; rather, they claimed, Jesus was an itinerant sage. The seminar also did not accept Jesus's miracles

---

21. Renan, *Vie de Jésus*, 4, 28, author's translation.
22. Boyarin, *Jewish Gospels*, and *Border Lines*.

as historical, and voted on which of his sayings were original to him.[23] Although the Jesus Seminar is no longer active, their questions have not disappeared. As recent scholarship has focused more on oral transmission and memory studies in relationship to biblical texts, however, some aspects of New Testament descriptions of Jesus have been reaffirmed. Even with little data from outside the New Testament, readers who understand elements of contemporary historiographical methods affirm the existence of this first-century Jewish man who walked the paths of Galilee and Judea. Further, New Testament writers' declarations that Jesus is the Son of God who rose from the dead continue to ring true for the Christian communities who have through centuries experienced resurrection power.

Beyond historical matters, however, other modern developments challenged the thinking of Bible readers. Throughout its ancient texts, the Bible had offered images that always could intersect with questions of philosophers and scientists in all times and cultures. The Bible opened with stirring descriptions of God as creator of the universe and everything in it. In the first creation story, God began by creating light. On the second day, God separated waters by means of a dome (Gen 1:7). English translations of this word have varied, from "firmament," to "sky," to "vault," or "dome," but the image the Genesis writers used came from a three-tiered view of the world: the earth on which humans lived, a realm below the ground, and a realm above the sky. This worldview was quite similar to that also described in ancient Babylonian and Egyptian documents. Biblical writers based their language about God's creative work on this three-tiered view, for example when the psalmist declared that God "set the earth on its foundations, so that it shall never be shaken" (Ps 104:5).

A more complex concept of the heavens, however, was emerging in late antiquity. Greeks, Romans, Egyptians, and Persians had all measured planetary and astral movements, and their sky maps placed Earth at the center, with higher and higher concentric circles surrounding it. Ascents into the heavens were reported in Hellenistic writings, a worldview Paul shared when he described a person (himself?) who was "caught up into the third heaven" (2 Cor 12:2). Although a few ancient Greek astronomers challenged that geocentric hypothesis, it dominated in most writings from New Testament times.

Nevertheless, observers did not stop observing and measuring heavenly movements, and a new perspective was suggested by fifteenth-century

---

23. Okoye, "Jesus and the Jesus Seminar."

clergyman Nicholas Copernicus. Copernicus had read both the Greek philosopher Aristotle and interpretations of his work by medieval Spanish Muslim philosopher Ibn Rushd. Copernicus measured and recorded planetary movement, and just before he died, published a work laying out the thesis that the Earth was not at the center, but rather part of a system orbiting the sun. Although some church leaders expressed an early interest in Copernicus's proposal, upheavals during the Reformation led to ecclesiastical resistance. Fifty years later, the astronomer Galileo used improvements in telescope technology for further astronomical study. He was first warned, then condemned to lifelong house arrest, for detailing heliocentric theories similar to those of Copernicus, because authorities thought that they contradicted Scripture. The account of Joshua commanding the sun to stand still was cited in Galileo's trial. Despite this opposition, however, observers continued to develop further advanced measurements of planetary and other cosmic movement. And some of these observers kept trying to articulate how God was at work behind such movement.

> *9.5 English mathematician Isaac Newton (1642–1727), famous for his explanation of the Laws of Motion, also pursued research on the solar system. In his* Principles of Mathematics, *he argued for a divine Creator as the source of heliocentric movement.*
>
> The six primary Planets are revolv'd about the Sun, in circles concentric with the Sun, and with motions directed towards the same parts and almost in the same plane. Ten Moons are revolv'd about the Earth, Jupiter and Saturn, in circles concentric with them, with the same direction of motion, and nearly in the planes of the orbits of those Planets. But it is not to be conceived that mere mechanical causes could give birth to so many regular motions . . . . This most beautiful System of the Sun, Planets and Comets, could only proceed from the counsel and dominion of an intelligent and powerful being. And if the fixed Stars are the centers of other like systems, these being form'd by the like wise counsel, must be all subject to the dominion of One; especially, since the light of the fixed Stars is of the same nature with the light of the Sun, and from every system light passes into all the other systems. And lest the systems of the fixed Stars should, by their gravity, fall on each other mutually, he hath placed those Systems at immense distances one from another. This Being governs all things, not as the soul of the world, but as Lord over all.[24]

---

24. Newton, "Extract from 'General Scholium,'" §3–4.

HOW HAVE MODERN DISCOVERIES IMPACTED UNDERSTANDINGS

In recent centuries, technological advancements have expanded knowledge about the universe far beyond observations about the Earth's relationship to the sun. At the end of the twentieth century, a Vatican court overturned the verdict against Galileo, declaring that the inquisitors at his trial were "incapable of dissociating faith from an age-old cosmology."[25] In 2022, the James Webb Space telescope offered pictures of "ancient light emitted by galaxies as they were forming billions of years ago in the infancy of the cosmos."[26]

Not only the heavens but also the natural phenomena of Earth elicited the curiosity of scientists, whose observations called for theological responses. During the Middle Ages, Persian philosopher Ibn Sina, commenting on Aristotle's writing on minerals, updated ancient perspectives on how mountains were formed. Chinese scientists recorded fossilized shells found on a mountain far from the ocean. For Europeans, similar discoveries gave rise to questions about how observable geological phenomena lined up with biblical accounts. An English theologian and mathematician in the eighteenth century argued that the Genesis flood account explained the formations in rock strata. In the nineteenth century Charles Darwin, based in part on his study of fossils collected while traveling in South America, hypothesized that all living creatures descended from a common ancestor.

Other researchers uncovered evidence of prehistoric human-like species. In the late nineteenth century, fossil remains of a species, named Homo erectus, were uncovered in Indonesia and dated to a million years old. In 1974, anthropologists exploring geological formations in northern Ethiopia uncovered an even older erect hominid skeleton, possibly three million years old. The dates assigned to these skeletons were based on analysis of the layers of volcanic ash that surrounded them. The evident age of the Earth, of life forms on the Earth, and particularly of creatures that were likely predecessors to modern humans seemed to contradict a straightforward reading of Genesis creation accounts.

Responses of Bible readers to these developments over the past two hundred years have varied, from angry refutation of any claims against a literal reading of biblical texts to respectful dialogue with some scientists. Theologians recalled that ancient Christians such as Augustine had, in fifth-century North Africa, declared that the Genesis creation accounts were

---

25. Sánchez de Toca, "Never Ending Story," 102.
26. Achenbach, "NASA Unveils First Images."

spiritual rather than literal descriptions. And as contemporary research continued to draw on Darwin's theories, many people admitted that there existed "a compelling body of evidence for organic evolution, i.e. evidence that life has unfolded over a long time, as a tree with many branches and many 'missing' branches ... with Homo sapiens appearing only recently."[27]

Modern believers seeking for a way to both uphold the truth of biblical accounts and to make a place for scientific evidence have evolved a variety of terms to talk about this evidence. Darwinian theories are known as "macroevolution," while "microevolution" describes the small genetic variations easily visible to researchers. For some, "theistic evolution" names the proposal that God initiated creation into which God built evolutionary processes. "Progressive creationism" refers to the idea that God created over and over, bringing to life through the millennia the different forms discovered in research, and "fiat creationism" describes the belief that "God created everything as it is now, in one instant."[28] Some people of faith, especially in the United States, still cling to readings of the Genesis accounts based on fiat creationism. But early in the twenty-first century, a broad spectrum of American religious leaders, including Christians and Jews, prepared open letters to their communities advocating a different approach.

> 9.6 *Christian clergy letter excerpt*: Within the community of Christian believers there are areas of dispute and disagreement, including the proper way to interpret Holy Scripture. While virtually all Christians take the Bible seriously and hold it to be authoritative in matters of faith and practice, the overwhelming majority do not read the Bible literally, as they would a science textbook. Many of the beloved stories found in the Bible—the Creation, Adam and Eve, Noah and the ark—convey timeless truths about God, human beings, and the proper relationship between Creator and creation expressed in the only form capable of transmitting these truths from generation to generation.[29]

> 9.7 *Jewish clergy letter excerpt*: The Bible is the primary source of spiritual inspiration and of values for us and for many others, though not everyone, in our society. It is, however, open to interpretation, with some taking the creation account and other content literally and some preferring a figurative understanding. It is

---

27. Broom and Mann, "Creationism vs Evolution," 18.
28. Tidmore, "Progressive Creationism," 79–80.
29. Wikipedia, "Clergy Letter Project," §5.

possible to be inspired by the religious teachings of the Bible while not taking a literalist approach and while accepting the validity of science including the foundational concept of evolution.[30]

In the twenty-first century, scientists, historians, and biblical scholars still have much to discuss. Sharp disagreement as well as friendly discourse can be heard across both scholarly journals and social media posts. Astrophysicists peering into the depths of the universe have begun to find forms of expression that share the wonderings of theologians. Writes one theologian-physicist: "Surely there has to be a boundary to our knowledge, and not every question that can be posed can be answered. It is quite remarkable, however, that we have made it to the edge of the universe and the beginning of time. Now that we are there, we discover that scientists and theologians are asking identical questions and even talking to each other."[31]

Further, as the urgent climate crisis on Planet Earth has become evident to everyone, believers from many disciplines again wonder how to affirm and uphold the biblical claim that God made everything good.[32] English professor Debra Rienstra calls on people of faith to see God's creative plan within the biological principle of refugia, "a biological term describing places of shelter where life endures in times of crisis, such as a volcanic eruption, fire, or stressed climate."[33] This insight may remind contemporary readers of biblical metaphors of seed and stump, of tree and river in the new earth, and perhaps direct our energy in that direction (Gen 1:11; Isa 11:1; Rev 22:1–2).

In our final chapter, we will consider how not only the explosion of human knowledge but also the dramatic diversity of identities among readers have shaped interpretations of the Bible's words.

---

30. Wikipedia, "Clergy Letter Project," §9.
31. Giberson, "Cosmos from Nothing?," 25.
32. Kirchhoffer, "How Ecology Can Save the Life of Theology."
33. Rienstra, *Refugia Faith*, book description.

Chapter 10

How Does the Bible Still Speak, and to Whom?

The Bible is one of the most translated books in human history. Portions of Scripture have been rendered into over three thousand languages, and at present there are nearly seven hundred modern translations of the complete Bible. So, no one argues that many people think it worth the time, effort, and money to make the Bible widely available. For centuries, Christians and Jews have studied Scripture, and in it they have heard God's word to them, even when it is hard to explain how that happens. Faithful readers have spent their lives not only reading, but also memorizing, commenting on, and trying to live by the counsel of the Bible.

Most people agree that the Bible is a religious book, whether or not they have read it, and either agreed or disagreed with its contents. The Bible's importance in faith communities is the foundation for the title that comparative religion scholars have bestowed on Jews, Christians, and Muslims; how these communities view the Bible and the Qur'an make them "people of the book." As we have seen, Christians built their Bible on the Jewish Tanakh. The Qur'an, though it has much that is unique to it, also reflects on portions of the Jewish and Christian Scriptures.

For centuries, the Bible appeared in the format of a book between two covers. Recently, more people access the Scripture on an app, through graphics, or on film.[1] No matter how we access the Bible, however, many

---

1. Since 1979, the Jesus Film Project has distributed a film based on a harmony of the four canonical Gospels. According to JFP reports, this film "is available in more than 2,000

readers today wonder more about what it really means than about the format in which they access it. In what follows, we will explore recent ways that people who accept the Bible as authority or guide have tried to understand what it is saying.

Two terms that shape efforts at determining biblical meaning are "inspiration" and "interpretation." The first word, "inspiration," is the basis for the claim that the Bible is God's word. The word "interpretation" describes the daily human experience of processing information. As we saw in chapter 8, across centuries people have developed a variety of interpretational strategies for the Bible, and understandings of the text have evolved alongside changes in language, culture, and technology. In the past century, biblical interpretation has become richer, more complicated, and at times troubling, as readers of diverse perspectives tangle with the text in diverse settings.

At the start of interpretation, people must recognize how much they actually know about the Bible. Even people who have not read the Bible may know a bit about some biblical characters. The figure of Moses is familiar in some cultures, and most people have some kind of mental picture of Jesus. Images of Mary, Jesus's mother, are also widespread. Within the English-speaking world, people also use expressions and ideas taken from the Bible. For example, a friend might intervene when someone is being blamed for wrong-doing, warning against "casting the first stone." Or a stranger who goes out of the way to help a traveler stranded by the road with a flat tire is described as "a good Samaritan."

These phrases entered into English usage through the influence of the seventeenth-century King James Version. The translation had a wide impact because it was published after the printing press was widely available, and was distributed throughout Europe as religious wars between Catholics and Protestants began to ebb. The King James Version was also one of the first major texts in modern rather than medieval English, thus carried around the world with military and missionary explorers. So comparative study of religions or ancient history and culture, as well as famous characters and key phrases and ideas, make this collection of writings at least partly familiar for many audiences.

However, for centuries before modern-language Bibles were in use, people who listened to Scripture and found its words useful did not focus on how to interpret what they heard and knew. From the time the biblical writings were sung around a fire; written on scrolls; edited, copied and

---

languages and has been seen in every country in the world" (https://www.jesusfilm.org/).

translated, people reflected on their own stories and struggles because they recognized echoes in biblical phrases. Judahites living in exile in Babylon renewed their hope when they heard the words, "Comfort, O comfort my people, says your God" (Isa 40:1). Later, somewhere in the Roman Empire, a preacher exhorted believers to "run with perseverance the race that is set before us, looking to Jesus" (Heb 12:1). Hearing this encouragement, the gathered community determined to keep coming together despite threats.

Theologians often cite a singular New Testament adjective to describe those people's experiences, as well as the Bible's self-understanding. That descriptor, "God-breathed" (*theopneustos*), appears only once in the New Testament, to describe the *written* text (2 Tim 3:16). The idea of God's active Spirit at work, however, was much older. In the languages of the Bible, the words for "spirit" can also mean "breath" or "wind." The poet of the first creation account described a wind or spirit from God moving over the formless deep (Gen 1:2) before God spoke light into existence. New Testament writers frequently added the adjective "holy" to describe the presence and action of God's Spirit. The earliest account of Jesus's baptism, to describe the visible sign of God's presence, offered the simile of a figure descending "like a dove" (Matt 3:16). Luke, when he recorded Jesus reading the Isaiah scroll in the synagogue, noted that the text for the day proclaimed that "the Spirit of the Lord" had empowered the prophet. Then Jesus added, "Today this scripture has been fulfilled" (Luke 4:18–21).

The word "inspiration" is built on the root word "spirit," and, broadly speaking, inspiration can describe both divine and human activity. Many people recount times when something pushed them to act. For example, a reflective citizen says, "After I watched the documentary on food insecurity, I was inspired to write to my member of Congress." And audiences frequently observe musicians as they perform, artists who display their work in public, and athletes who play with brilliance, calling them inspired.

Yet those who throughout the centuries have made the Bible part of their life also experience God's presence and action. The first-century Jewish philosopher Philo described this experience, as he explained how manna for Israelites in the desert was part of God's gift of Sabbath: "Moses, now being inspired, declared to his people in an oracle which was borne testimony to by a visible sign from heaven. And the sign was this. A small portion of food descended from the air on the previous days, but a double portion on the day before the seventh day."[2]

2. Philo, *Life of Moses*, in *Works of Philo* 2.264–65.

A contemporary to the writer of John's Gospel, Philo also used the same term as the evangelist, *logos*, to name the divine gift of reason. For Philo, *logos* was at the intersection of God's revelation and God's word.[3] The Gospel of John used this same term to echo the opening line of Genesis, "In the beginning was the *logos*." Many Bibles capitalize John's "Word," and commentators agree that John was describing Jesus Christ as the Word who was with God at the beginning (John 1:1–2). John moved in a different direction from Philo, though, when he added that "the Word became flesh" (John 1:14).

Most Christian churches teach that Jesus was a fully human Jewish man during his first-century life in Galilee and Judea. They also proclaim that Jesus Christ is the most complete revelation of God to humanity. This assertion, that Jesus Christ is the Word made flesh, is known theologically as the doctrine of the incarnation. Efforts to articulate this claim through the centuries have been many and complicated. When the doctrine of the incarnation intersects with the belief that the divine Word also comes to us through marks printed on Bible pages, or blinking at us on our screens, understandings of inspiration become more complicated, but also richer.

Thus, from the beginning, hearers and readers have formed a variety of explanations of how the Bible is God's word. These explanations also influence how readers approach biblical interpretation. Ancient and medieval theologians often used spiritual or allegorical readings of God's word, especially for hard-to-understand passages in the Old Testament, as we saw in chapter 8. God's commands for warfare seemed unlike the God of Jesus to many early Christians. Origen explained: "We must add that it was after the advent of Jesus that the inspiration of the prophetic words and the spiritual nature of Moses's law came to light."[4] Often the explanations that those early Christian interpreters derived came to be understood as methods or rules. But those early readers, rather than focusing on rubrics, were shaping their practice of discerning Christ within any text they heard.[5]

Jesus's teachings as recorded in the New Testament were usually interpreted quite straightforwardly. North African theologian Tertullian, explaining why Christians could not be soldiers, referred to Jesus's words about serving God or the emperor, adding: "Although a centurion had

---

3. Lévy, "Philo of Alexandria."

4. Origen, *On First Principles* 4.1.6.

5. Thanks to Zachary Spidel and Andrea Dalton Saner for pointing out the importance of this understanding of spiritual reading of the Bible.

believed, still the Lord afterward, in disarming Peter, unbelted every soldier."[6] Bishop Athanasius, in his biography of the Egyptian monk Antony, described the young man listening in church to the gospel when Jesus commanded the rich young ruler to sell everything and give to the poor. "As though the reading had been directed especially to him, Antony immediately left the church and gave to the townspeople the property he had from his forebears."[7] Clare of Assisi, a medieval Italian nun, wrote to a noble friend: "You know . . . that a camel will be able to pass through the eye of a needle before a rich person ascends to the kingdom of heaven. These are the reasons why you disposed of your clothing, I mean your worldly wealth."[8]

With the rise of modernity, however, for some readers the intimate relationship between the word of Scripture and Christ as Word faded into the background. Rather, "skeptics and apologists alike came to see the Bible's authority as derivative of and conditional upon its historical, scientific, or existential accuracy."[9] From the eighteenth century on, discussions raged each time new information challenged traditional thinking about the Bible as God's word. In response to several centuries of such modern debates, early in the twentieth century a group of American Christian apologists published ninety essays titled *The Fundamentals: A Testimony to the Truth*. This collection, covering a wide range of topics, was motivated by opposition to higher biblical criticism, their term for modern scholarship's efforts to verify the Bible's stories and manuscripts. These essays claimed that "it is impossible to secure the religious infallibility of the Bible—which is all the objector regards as necessary—if we exclude Bible history from the sphere of its inspiration."[10] Throughout the last century, especially in the United States, believers influenced by these essays have repeated their affirmations of the Bible's authority. A 1978 meeting of Fundamentalist scholars declared: "Being wholly and verbally God-given, Scripture is without error or fault in all its teaching, no less in what it states about God's acts in creation,

---

6. Tertullian, *On Idolatry* 19.

7. Athanasius, *Life of Antony* 2.

8. Clare of Assisi, "First Letter to Agnes of Prague," 263.

9. Telford Work, "Authority of Scripture," in *NIDB* 1:352–53.

10. Gray, "Inspiration of the Bible," in *Fundamentals*. For the complete text of *Fundamentals*, see https://www.blueletterbible.org/Comm/torrey_ra/fundamentals/20.cfm.

about the events of world history, and about its own literary origins under God, than in its witness to God's saving grace in individual lives."[11]

Other Christians who keep the Bible at the center in their life as faith communities nevertheless articulate different claims. Douglass defines several key terms that characterize contemporary "evangelical/Anabaptists." Beginning with the foundation that biblical inspiration means, "at a minimum, that God has had some kind of role in [the Bible's] creation," he proposes a spectrum. At the one end is the assertion that human abilities, illuminated by God, created the Bible. At the other is the claim that "the human involvement in the creation of the texts can be related to a secretary taking dictation." For Douglass, neither end of this spectrum is satisfactory, leading to several intermediary views. One, "verbal plenary inspiration," accepts the involvement of human authors but declares that "the words that are written are God's chosen words." A second, "dynamic" view is that "God inspired the authors of Scripture rather than the words." A third view proposes to deal with problems that arise for many modern readers. In this view, God "accommodated his revelation or self-disclosure so that it could be received by the people he was addressing." Finally, a "general view" of inspiration understands God "as involved in the formation of the Bible but not necessarily directly and certainly not meticulously."[12]

While faith communities have struggled to reassert their commitments to the Bible's authority, within academic biblical scholarship the diversity of participants has also dramatically expanded. For some scholars, analyzing literary structures in the Bible is more useful in clarifying the what the Bible says than fact-checking them against historical and scientific data. Thus, for example, rhetoricians observe the apostle Paul using methods prescribed in Greco-Roman rhetoric manuals when he boasts or uses irony in his Corinthian correspondence. Theories from psychology, sociology, anthropology, and economics have brought other new insights to Bible students. The socio-anthropological concept of honor and shame elucidates what is occurring in biblical stories, when researchers observe behaviors in biblical stories that are referenced in other ancient cultures. For example the showdown between Jeremiah and Hananiah, two prophets in the last days of the kingdom of Judah, can now be read as an honor challenge. Both prophets

---

11. Gospel Coalition, "Chicago Statement on Biblical Inerrancy."

12. Douglass, "Current Evangelical/Anabaptist Perspectives." For a fuller discussion of the background to evangelical understanding of biblical inspiration, see Messmer, "Inspiration, Authority, and Inerrancy of Scripture," 294–315.

proclaimed the word of YHWH, but with very different messages. Thus the one whose message was false would suffer loss of honor.[13]

The *New Cambridge Guide to Biblical Interpretation* (2022) surveys this dramatic expansion of interpretational practices. In addition to a critical retrospective on historical biblical criticism the *Guide* offers articles on liberationist, postcolonial, feminist, LGBTI/Queer, and ecological theories that have been applied in reading the Bible. This explosion of approaches challenges scholars to stay informed about what is happening in their field, and has often fragmented conversations about how and for whom the Bible speaks.

Contemporary faith communities have not avoided the challenges that come from these diverse approaches, but have also found them enlightening. Around the world, within groups long ignored or hidden from academic scholars, readers now claim their own locations as fruitful interpretational settings. Of course, such diversity of contextual readings is not new. Ancient churches who worshiped in Latin differed from those worshiping in Greek over how to interpret what the Bible claimed about Jesus. Medieval Europeans clamored for Bible translations in languages ordinary people could understand. Clusters of nineteenth-century Swedish dissenters gathered for home Bible studies, even though such meetings were illegal. And enslaved Africans in the Americas pointed out the corruption of biblical interpretation that defended the enslavement of human beings.

> *10.1 In 1852, abolitionist Frederick Douglass, who had escaped from enslavement, asked in a famous speech, "What to the slave is the Fourth of July?" To answer his question, Douglass quoted the Bible to show that White American Christians had ignored the Bible's teaching.*
>
> [Religion in this country is] not that *"pure and undefiled religion"* which is from above, and which is *"first pure, then peaceable, easy to be entreated,* full of mercy and good fruits, *without partiality, and without hypocrisy."* But a religion which favors the rich against the poor; which exalts the proud above the humble; which divides mankind into two classes, tyrants and slaves; which says to the man in chains, *stay there*; and to the oppressor, *oppress on*; it is a religion which may be professed and enjoyed by all the robbers and enslavers of mankind; it makes God a respecter of persons, denies his fatherhood of the race, and tramples in the dust the great truth of the brotherhood of man. All this we affirm to be true

---

13. Bartusch, "From Honor Challenge to False Prophecy."

of the popular church, and the popular worship of our land and nation—a religion, a church, and a worship which, on the authority of inspired wisdom, we pronounce to be an abomination in the sight of God.[14]

Still, the twentieth century was a time when important new communities of biblical study emerged. Nations in Africa and Asia gained independence from colonial domination; the civil rights movement fought for the rights of Black people in the United States; Roman Catholic leaders in Latin America resisted harsh military dictators; women demanded equal rights at home, work, and in church; and citizens around the world protested the testing of nuclear weapons. These movements, aided by new communication technologies, brought more voices into the conversation. Taking note of these voices, some biblical scholars are seeking to learn from those without formal training, as well as from different classes, ethnic groups, and genders. The idea that the locations of readers must be a starting point for interpretation became widespread. Thus contextual biblical scholars seek to join day laborers, unhoused people, low-wage workers, and persons living with mental health challenges, to read and interpret the Bible.[15] Such efforts reflect the hope and promise that the Bible shows God's way to resist evil and love one another even in the midst of injustice and suffering.

Taking the responses of diverse readers into account, however, has not been easy for faith communities. Traditional interpretation methods begin with the understanding that God's word is a priori, and human response is secondary. The intersection of God's voice and human response in personal reading has long been a powerful part of talking about what the Bible means. In public worship and preaching, leaders have assumed that God's word comes first, and its force must override human experience. Thus, when people demand the right not only to listen where they sit but to allow their locations to shape how they interpret, ecclesial authorities often become uncomfortable. Observations about what the Bible says about economic class, race, or gender, or about how to respond to violence, sometimes frighten those who have lived in stable and comfortable worlds. But many readers have personal experiences to question why God would command people to kill all their enemies, or slaves to obey their masters, or

14. Douglass, "What to the Slave?"
15. West, "Reading the Bible with the Marginalised."

women to be silent in the assembly, or whether God intends wealth as a sign of divine blessing. In scholarly terms, working on such ideas involves the discipline of hermeneutics, that is, the study of methods and theories of interpretation. In the face of critiques about how the Bible has been preached to enslaved people, women, or economically stressed people, some adopt a "hermeneutics of suspicion." They may even decide that they can no longer find a good word in the Bible. Even those who work within a "hermeneutics of trust" often struggle with parts of Scripture.[16] In addition to examples in 10.1 above and 10.2, following, excerpts from interpreters who draw from both hermeneutics are included at the end of this section.

> 10.2 *Justo González is a Cuban-American historical theologian and Methodist elder. One chapter in his book* Santa Biblia, *"Mestizaje and Mulatez," explores his perspective on a famous Bible story, as read by of people of Spanish, Indigenous, and African identities in the Americas.*
>
> I wish I had a dollar for every time I have heard a preacher say that Saul gave up his Hebrew name, and took the name of Paul, when he became a Christian. I have even heard eloquent sermons as to how *Saul* the persecutor fell down to earth, and up rose *Paul* the Christian, *Paul* the missionary, *Paul* the apostle.
>
> It is very pretty, very traditional, and very inspiring. The only problem is that it isn't true. Read the book of Acts again. [All the mentions are of Saul, until] almost surreptitiously, in Acts 13:9, Luke refers to "Saul, also known as Paul." And from that point on, throughout the entire book of Acts, Saul has become Paul.
>
> The fact of the matter is that Saul, like many others of his time, had two names. One was the name in his traditional culture—in this case, Judaism. He was named Saul after the great leader of his own tribe of Benjamin. But he also had a Roman name, a name for use outside of Jewish circles. That name was Paul. Saul/Paul was a cultural *mestizo*.[17]

Many Bible readers now think carefully about how biblical truths expand and challenge us when we join a widening community of interpreters. The Lausanne Movement, a worldwide missionary body, proclaimed in a 2010 statement: "We affirm that the Bible is the final written word of God, not

---

16. Gorman, *Elements of Biblical Exegesis*, 154–58.
17. González, *Santa Biblia*, 80–81.

surpassed by any further revelation, but we also rejoice that the Holy Spirit illumines the minds of God's people so that the Bible continues to speak God's truth in fresh ways to people in every culture."[18] Another four-year conversation among American and British scholars and pastors came to a consensus about listening to new voices in biblical interpretation.

> 10.3 *Published as* The Art of Reading Scripture, *thirteen scholars and pastors representing several Christian traditions expressed their agreements in nine theses. Each thesis comes with questions that remain open for the group. In thesis eight, they address some realities of belonging to a community of diverse readers.*
>
> Christians need to read the Bible in dialogue with diverse others outside the church. There is a special need for Christians to read Scripture in respectful conversation with Jews, who also serve the one God and read the same texts that we call the Old Testament within a different hermeneutical framework. There are also diverse others to whom we need to listen and from whom we need to learn. This includes critics who charge us with ideological captivity rather than fidelity to God. *For ongoing discussion*: How do we pursue the tasks of learning (again) to read Scripture faithfully in the church while also being in dialogue with those outside? How should we understand and engage people who find themselves, in some sense, simultaneously inside and outside a fragmented church?[19]

Often the discourse about both inspiration and interpretation takes place in intellectual environments where analysis and content are central. However, the Bible is also at the heart of many communities who gather together to hear it in worship and study. Throughout the centuries, faithful people have found corporate reading of Scripture enlivening and useful, offering rich insights into God's purposes as they listen in their own contexts for guidance. It is true, as history provides tragic evidence, that peoples and nations claiming Scripture as their guide have committed and defended terrible acts. So, the best evidence of what it means to claim Scripture as inspired comes when communities try to "do justice, love mercy, and walk humbly with God" (Mic 6:8). Living out what the Bible proclaims can both shape

---

18. Lausanne Movement, "Cape Town Commitment," §6.
19. Davis and Hays, *Art of Reading Scripture*, 4–5.

personal choices and, in community and corporate settings, have political, economic, and cultural impacts.

For sixteenth-century Anabaptists, living in obedience to Scripture meant refusing to take up the sword, even in self-defense. Anabaptists thought that this nonresistance was clearly taught in the New Testament, but other Christians argued that such an interpretation did not take the whole Bible into account. Nevertheless, within decades, Anabaptists fell into schism when they disagreed over whether the Bible required one spouse to shun the other if the community had banned their partner. This move exposed the harm that could be caused by a rigid understanding of biblical obedience. Recently, ethicist Corbin-Reuschling calls for a fuller approach to biblical obedience when facing such difficult matters. She encourages readers to attend to "the narrative context of the entire canon of scripture, along with the necessary elements of conscience formation, moral agency, and skills in ethical deliberation."[20] African-American theologian Bennett encourages "Africentric Pentecostal moral decision-making" that reads Scripture not as "a comprehensive ethics manual," but "an encounter with The Radical Presence, i.e., being in touch with something bigger and far more precious and powerful than the Bible, as the ultimate source for delineating good and bad deeds."[21]

Beyond the hallways of debate, from ancient times to the present, centering the reading of and preaching from the Bible in worship has been essential for biblical interpretation. When Jewish communities gather for services, those who are called up to read the Torah begin and end with blessings praising God for giving them this word, and for "planting eternal life in our midst."[22] Roman Catholics proclaim in their 1992 catechism: "Through all the words of Sacred Scripture, God speaks only one single Word, his one Utterance in whom he expresses himself completely. For this reason, the Church has always venerated the Scriptures as she venerates the Lord's Body. She never ceases to present to the faithful the bread of life, taken from the one table of God's Word and Christ's Body."[23]

In many Christian services the Bible is read out loud, after which the reader proclaims: "The word of God for the people of God." And the community replies, "Thanks be to God!" East declares that this practice should

---

20. Corbin-Reuschling, "'Trust and Obey,'" 72.
21. Bennett, "Bible and Africentric Pentecostal Moral Decision-Making," 15.
22. Millgram, *Jerusalem Curiosities*, 8.
23. "Catechism," art. 3.1.

remind Christian that the Bible and its entire human history are God's gift to God's people. He writes: "The church is, in a more than nominal sense, the author of Scripture. The church's founders composed it; her predecessors preserved it; her councils canonized it; her leaders authorize its use in the present. To stand in a relation of grateful reception to God for the gift of Scripture, therefore, is also to stand in a relation of grateful reception to God's people."[24]

This rapid overview may overwhelm us with the wide variety of ways that believers have thought about the inspiration of the Bible and outlined methods of interpreting it. We have noted in various parts of the story how humans have misinterpreted the Bible, discovered new data that confused them, forgot what they heard, or deliberately disobeyed the Bible's clear commands. Some abandon the Bible completely, are never enticed to open its covers, or do not even understand why the Bible is relevant.

Yet the Spirit of God that hovered over the waters at creation and created humanity in God's image continues to move believers around the world.[25] Millennia ago, psalmists, linking God's first acts of creation to their own time, called out: "When you send forth your spirit, [all things] are created, and you renew the face of the ground" (Ps 104:30). Today, observant Jews recite that psalm every day. Christians too wait for and join in the creative work of God's Spirit. Whether in formal liturgies on Pentecost, or in the most intimate gatherings, we pray: "Come, Holy Spirit, fill the hearts of Thy faithful and kindle in them the fire of Thy love. Send forth Thy Spirit and they shall be created. And Thou shalt renew the face of the earth."[26]

As this chapter has demonstrated, the Bible continues to be read widely and interpreted from a variety of settings. The following excerpts offer additional illustrations of how contemporary biblical readers engage and wonder about Scripture.

> *Mitzi J. Smith is professor of New Testament at Columbia Theological Seminary in Decatur, Georgia. An African American scholar, she spent much of her career teaching in inner-city Detroit.*

---

24. East, "Is Scripture a Gift?," 17.

25. Clifton-Soderstrom, "Common Sense, Plain Sense."

26. Christian hymnal indices reveal hundreds of texts invoking the Spirit or Breath of God.

It is not enough to believe that God stands with or at the side of the oppressed. God has skin/flesh in the game. Thus, I take seriously Mary's self-identification as a δουλη (an enslaved female) in the birth narratives of the Gospel of Luke. Enslaved women birth enslaved infants, not free born babies. From this perspective, Mary's son, God's beloved, Jesus was born an enslaved male and navigated life in stigmatized flesh from birth to crucifixion. Jesus lived a precarious existence always under the threat of violence and oppression, and eventually dying a death reserved primarily for the criminalized and enslaved, by crucifixion.[27]

Jione Havea, a Tongan Methodist pastor, reflects on John the Baptist's call to repentance in light of his island nation's threatened disappearance due to climate change. Havea is a research fellow at Trinity Theological College, Auckland (Aotearoa), New Zealand.

Baptism becomes a ritual that welcomes the baptized into solidarity with communities—such as those in the Marshalls, Maohi Nui, Kiribati, Tuvalu, Papua, Fiji, and yonder—who continue to suffer from the legacies of war and the excrements of the human carbon civilization. The baptized will thus live the will and teachings of John the Baptist: "Whoever has two coats must share with anyone who has none; and whoever has food must do likewise" (Luke 3:11, NRSV). [Further], baptism does not remove or separate the baptized person from that person's context (the biblical understanding of what it means to be holy). Rather, baptism is an opportunity for one to advocate, resist, and protest on behalf of those who are wronged. John instructs us: "Collect no more than the amount prescribed for you." "Do not extort money from anyone by threats or false accusation, and be satisfied with your wages" (Luke 3:13, 14; NRSV).[28]

Jacqueline Grey is an ordained pastor in the Australian Christian Churches and a member of the Society for Pentecostal Studies.

What is particularly interesting, in light of the dominant Assyrian ideology and emphasized by a post-colonial reading, is the sense of movement in this poem of Isaiah 2:1–5. The first half of the poem is dominated by movement towards Zion, while the second half reflects movement out from Zion. Rivers stream to Zion in the Psalms, but in this passage it is people. The nations come to the

---

27. Smith, "Womanist Activist Approach," 40.
28. Havea, "Holy Baptism, Troubled Waters," 9.

mountain in peace (rather than to attack) and voluntarily. A link between the nations streaming to Jerusalem and Jeremiah 51:44 suggests a reversal of the reality of exile; Judah and the nations will no longer stream to Babylon as captives but stream to Jerusalem as willing students.... Christianity is not, and was not, a European movement nor a colonial movement. Instead it finds its missionary origins in West Asia among the colonized of the Roman Empire. The restoration of missionary origins from a colonial centre to the periphery can be helpful in many ways.[29]

James Alison grew up in an Evangelical Anglican family in England, and became a Catholic at the age of eighteen. He was ordained priest in 1988. Having lived with the Dominican Order between 1981 and 1995, Alison now works as an itinerant preacher, lecturer, and retreat giver. When not on the road, he lives in Madrid, Spain. In this article excerpt, Alison responds to a request from the journal Christian Century, *to comment on "how my mind has changed."*

All students at the Jesuit Theology Faculty [where I studied in Brazil] also had to be involved in pastoral work. We were required to learn to think about what we were doing, first sociologically and anthropologically and then theologically. Our teachers wanted to ensure that we were not tempted to imagine that learning theology was possible anywhere except face to face with the suffering servant. McCabe [a professor I had studied with in England] had instructed me, "James, whenever you write anything theological, stop and ask yourself: Yes, but is it true?" St. Ignatius's companions now wanted me to ask, in a way with which McCabe would wholeheartedly have concurred, "Where in all of this is Christ crucified?" And so AIDS became the constant crucible for my learning.

AIDS as it was before 1994, with death so fast and agonies so cruel but also loves so poignant, shame so rampant, backstories so bizarre, poverty so omnipresent, and families so riven that even the terrified and self-obsessed person that I was began to be pulled into the orbit of the suffering servant. And by this I mean that I began to glimpse that the suffering servant was not me. I am not the victim here. The center is radiantly elsewhere, and I am, thank God, peripheral to it. Never had I been so alive as in the face of this emergency. Is it shocking to say this? Only in the AIDS trenches (a First World War metaphor not taken lightly) could the full measure of the drastic inner logic of my fear, my shame, my sense of worthlessness, and my semi-suicidal dance with death and danger

---

29. Grey, "Through the Looking Glass," 32, 36.

come alive and meet its match in the shames and glories of the lives and deaths of those I accompanied. The utter privilege of being a priest accompanying people with AIDS, while learning theology at graced hands, was what allowed Jesus finally to apply balm to the drasticity that had so precociously ripped through the heart of a nine-year-old [gay] boy.[30]

April Klaassen-Brown is a 100 percent Cree from Thunderchild Nation in northern Saskatchewan. As a child she was adopted by a Mennonite family of German heritage, and spent several years with them on a missionary assignment in the Democratic Republic of the Congo, where she became friends with the author. She wrote this remembrance in October 2023.

Today my family lays my oldest sister to rest. I didn't get to know her much at all. Our lives were intertwined though through getting to know my biological family again. . . . Loss of family, loss of family moments, loss of relationship. It's a tough thing to walk through when it wasn't a choice. BUT the Creator had a plan for my life which brought much healing through life experiences. I have learned that forgiveness opens the doors to deep, deep healing. I know without a shadow of doubt the Creator loves. HE LOVES. I have been reconnected to my family. This past week, my father's sister came and hugged me and gave me a kiss on the cheek. A little thing to someone perhaps but a huge but quiet wow to me. Another aunt sat with me and we laughed and laughed; she used to babysit me when I was a very wee one. She also kissed me on the cheek and with tears in her eyes, said she was so happy to see me again. I've sat with another sister and we've spoken at length about many things, reconnecting. My brother and his wife and their whole family, whom I've gotten to know so much better since we've found each again. It has been very good. How I ended up to be at this very time is really only God. Both my son Taran and I saw white owls this past week, each separately and we both knew what that meant. BUT I knew that I knew the Mercy of God was in that message. I know the Creator loved my sister; there was his seed of love planted in her when my parents walked in the strength and path of the Creator at one time. That seed of Love brings us together to remember her, who she was. We remember and love her children and grandchildren here with us now. I know in her heart she was proud of them. Love heals, Love restores, Love

---

30. Alison, "Brought to Life by Christ," 33–34.

builds up, Love conquers all, even death. The Creator sent his Son so we could be reunited with HIS Great and Mighty LOVE for us.

I love you Eileen. You were/are much loved by the Creator. "For I am convinced that neither death nor life, neither angels nor demons, neither the present nor the future, nor any powers, neither height nor depth, nor anything else in all creation, will be able to separate us from the love of God that is in Christ Jesus our Lord" (Rom 8:38–39).[31]

---

31. Personal communication, December 5, 2023.

Appendix A

Glossary

Apocalyptic: Term from the Greek word for "unveiling" or "revelation." In biblical literature, this adjective describes texts that were told by a seer-guide, used code language and numerological symbols, recounted fantastic visions, and described divinely directed battle. The term is often used in connection with the adjective "eschatological," which refers to things having to do with the end of time. While apocalyptic literature assumed the end of the history as known to its readers, it is frequently set within and refers to specific historical periods and events. Also used as a noun, "apocalypse."

Apocrypha: Jewish religious writings from the Second Temple period that are related to texts found in established biblical canons. Some early Christian writings are called New Testament apocrypha. Texts included in the Old Testament apocrypha by Protestants are called the Deuterocanon in Catholic and Orthodox churches. The original meaning of "apocrypha" is "hidden things," but in modern usage for many people it denotes "false writings."

BCE and *CE*: Dating system used by contemporary historians. BCE, or Before the Common Era, appeared in earlier literature with the acronym BC. CE, or Common Era, was traditionally noted as AD. BCE dates are listed in descending order, e.g., 800–750 BCE. CE dates are listed in ascending order, e.g., 1098–1179 CE.

Codex/codices: An early book format, used first by Christians in the third and fourth centuries CE. This method of collecting and copying written materials can be contrasted with the ancient and more formal scroll format.

Hasmoneans: The name taken by the Maccabean priestly family who successfully revolted against Hellenistic Seleucid rulers from Syria, in 167–160 BCE. When the Maccabean family claimed royal status in Judea, their dynasty became known as the Hasmoneans, ruling from 140–37 BCE. The name derives from an otherwise unknown historical ancestor of the family.

Hellenization: The broad infusion and imposition of Greek language, science, philosophy, and religion, throughout the eastern Mediterranean region, following the conquests of Alexander the Great (336–323 BCE). The spread of common, or Koine, Greek facilitated both imperial ambitions and broad exchange of ideas and practices. Greek influence remained powerful for centuries, although hellenization took on its own unique character in each region where it had an impact. The translation of the Hebrew Bible into Greek (Septuagint/LXX), and the fact that the entire New Testament was written in Greek, indicate the importance of this cultural history for the Bible.

Hermeneutics: Theories and methods of interpreting texts. Ancient popular usage linked the Greek term with the god Hermes, a messenger and mediator between gods and humans. Early study of hermeneutics was directed specifically at religious and philosophical texts because they were assumed to have meanings that required special skill to understand. In modern scholarship, hermeneutics can be focused on materials across the humanities.

Herod: Name of several kings who ruled Judea and other parts of Palestine during the first century CE. The founder of the family was Herod the Great, a client of the Roman Empire, who ruled Judea from 37 to 4 BCE, and was king at the time of the birth of Jesus. His descendants also played roles in the New Testament story. Herod Antipas ordered the death of John the Baptist. Herod Agrippa I imprisoned Peter (Acts 12) and Herod Agrippa II heard Paul's defense (Acts 25).

GLOSSARY

Hieroglyphics: Communication system used in ancient Egyptian monumental structures from the third millennium BCE. Hieroglyphics included some alphabetic symbols but was most recognized by its use of pictographs.

Israel: The name given by God to the patriarch Jacob in Gen 32, which later became the identifying name for the people of Israel or Israelites. Eventually, Israel also became the name of the northern kingdom, with Samaria as the capital. Ancient Israel and the Israelite people must be understood as different from the modern state of Israel, whose citizens are called Israelis.

Judah: The name of the southern kingdom centered in Jerusalem. During the Persian Empire (539–323 BCE), where Aramaic was the common language of the western part of the empire, Yehud was the name of the administrative province of what had been the kingdom of Judah. The territory came to be called Judea under Roman domination, and those whose origins were Judean were called *Ioudaioi*, transliterated into English as "Jews."

Masoretic Text/MT: The texts of the Hebrew Bible prepared, beginning in the ninth century CE, by rabbinic scribes known as the Masoretes. Their texts included careful markings to clarify spellings and readings, added to the Hebrew that had earlier been written only with consonants. These markings, in Hebrew *masora*, give the name to these manuscripts. The oldest Masoretic Text of the complete Hebrew Bible is the Leningrad Codex from the early eleventh century CE. Until the discovery of the Dead Sea Scrolls, all Protestant Bible versions were based on the MT.

Messiah/Christ: Title given to Jesus in the New Testament. Its use dates to the ancient practice of anointing the rulers of Israel to represent their assuming royal power. Messiah means "anointed one," and "Christ" is the Greek translation of the Hebrew word.

Ostraca (singular *ostracon*): Greek for pottery fragments, or sherds. Ostraca were used as writing material in the ancient world, likely for ordinary people with little access to formal media such as papyrus or parchment. Archeologists study found ostraca for inscriptions that might reveal additional information about a particular site.

Nicaea/Nicene: City in Asia Minor (Iznik in modern Turkey), where the first ecumenical council of Christian churches took place in 325 CE. An "ecumenical" council intended to include representatives from all regions where the church was present, in contrast to earlier regional councils. At the council a formal creed, or statement of belief, was worked out, in an effort to resolve disputes about how to describe the divinity of Jesus Christ. Nicene Christianity affirmed that Jesus and God were eternally of "one substance." Arian Christians argued that Jesus was God's first creation. Both groups drew on biblical statements, although the term "one substance" was problematic to almost everyone because it was not in the Bible.

Palestine: The name given by the Romans to the region that had been known as Judea, after the second Jewish revolt (132–35 CE). "Palestine" was a Latinized form of "Philistine," the biblical term for the coastal enemies of the early Israelites. During the Byzantine Empire, beginning in the sixth century until 1453 CE, Palestine was widely used as the name for the region. Under British colonial rule, the name Palestine again became prominent and, in 1948, was given to the portion of the region not allotted to the newly formed state of Israel.

Papyrus (plural *papyri*): A medium for writing common in the ancient Mediterranean. Papyri were made from strips of the papyrus reed growing in swampy regions in Egypt. "Papyrus" is also used to identify specific ancient manuscripts or fragments as, for example, Papyrus 46, a partial codex containing most of the Pauline letters.

Pseudepigrapha: Literally "falsely attributed writings," Jewish texts, primarily from the Second Temple period, that frequently used pseudonyms. Among the well-known examples of this broad group of writings are books such as 1 Enoch, which is quoted in the New Testament (Jude 1:14), 4 Ezra, and the Psalms of Solomon.

Qumran: A location near the Dead Sea, called Khirbet Qumran by archeologists. The site of an ancient community was excavated and continues to be referenced by scholars in relationship to a collection of ancient scrolls found in nearby caves. This vast collection of manuscripts and fragments are usually called the Dead Sea Scrolls, because many were found beyond Qumran, in other parts of the surrounding southern desert.

GLOSSARY

Sayings Source (Q): Name given by scholars to describe large blocks of parallel sayings of Jesus found in the Gospels of Matthew and Luke. This material is also called "Q," based on the German word for "source," *Quelle*. The discovery of manuscripts of the Gospel of Thomas, a collection of sayings of Jesus, led to proposals that Thomas was similar to the hypothetical Sayings Source. The Gospel of Thomas is available for study in Coptic, along with some Greek fragments, but no saying source manuscripts are known.

Second Temple period: Historical designation for the centuries from the Jewish return from Babylon in 535 BCE until the Roman destruction of Jerusalem in 70 CE. Early efforts to rebuild the temple are described in Ezra and Nehemiah. Herod the Great greatly enhanced this temple's size and architecture. This temple, described in the Gospels, was critiqued by Jesus.

Septuagint: Broad term describing the most ancient Greek translations of the Hebrew Bible, especially the Torah, carried out beginning in the 250s BCE. The term comes from the Latin form of the number seventy, written LXX, and indicating the story in the *Letter of Aristeas* that describes seventy-two scholars from Jerusalem who went to Egypt to prepare the translation. In modern editions the term "Septuagint" also includes all the Greek texts from the Tanakh and the Deuterocanon/Apocrypha.

Tanakh: The Jewish Bible, referred to by an acronym, Tanakh/TNK, is organized in three groups of texts: Torah (Pentateuch); Neviim (Prophets), the Former Prophets from Joshua through 2 Kings, and the Latter Prophets from Isaiah through Malachi; Ketubim (Writings), all the other books. The modern Jewish Tanakh contains twenty-four titles: the five books of the Torah, eight Prophets, and eleven Writings. First and Second Samuel, 1–2 Kings, the Book of the Twelve Minor Prophets, Ezra and Nehemiah, and 1–2 Chronicles are each counted as single books. The thirty-nine books of the Protestant Old Testament include these same writings.

Torah: In its first meaning, Hebrew for "law." Use of the word expanded to name the first five books of the Old Testament (see Tanakh), and beyond that to the extensive collection of writings that are the foundation of Jewish faith. Jewish practices and biblical interpretations are collected in the written (five books) and oral Torah, later rabbinic materials that form the Talmud.

APPENDIX A

YHWH: The Hebrew name of God, often called the tetragrammaton (four letters) by scholars. This name was given to Moses with the definition: "I AM WHO I AM" (Exod 3:14). In Jewish tradition by the time of Jesus, this divine name was considered too holy to be spoken. Because its earliest written form had no vowels, YHWH has been variously transliterated as Jehovah or Yahweh. Many modern Bible versions indicate the presence of YHWH with the word LORD (different from Lord).

Appendix B

Ancient History Comparative Dates

Egypt	Mesopotamia	Mediterranean	Israel/Palestine
Hieroglyphic writing developed 3000s BCE	Cuneiform writing developed 3000s BCE		
	Hammurabi law code ca. 1755 BCE		
Merneptah Stela 1208 BCE		Greek alphabet derived from Phoenician script ca. 1000 BCE	Kingdom of David/Solomon ca. 1000 BCE Ancient Hebrew in Phoenician script
Pharaoh Sheshonq invaded Judah 925 BCE		Works of Homer compiled 700s BCE	Northern-Southern Kingdoms split ca. 900 BCE
	Nineveh in Assyria destroyed by Babylon 612 BCE		Prophets Hosea, Amos, Isaiah Israel destroyed by Assyria 722 BCE

APPENDIX B

Egypt	Mesopotamia	Mediterranean	Israel/Palestine
	Judahite exiles in Babylon 586–538 BCE		Judah destroyed by Babylon 586 BCE
	Prophet Ezekiel		Prophet Jeremiah
Jewish community in Upper Egypt write letters to Jerusalem			
	Torah edited and compiled Hebrew written in Aramaic letters		Persian Empire ruled Palestine 550–329 BCE
Ptolemies rule, beginning 323 BCE		Alexander the Great campaigns 336–323 BCE	Seleucids rule from Syria, after defeat of Ptolemies 198 BCE
Translation of Septuagint Mid-3rd c. BCE			Maccabean Revolt begins 167 BCE
			Qumran community ca. 150 BCE–70 CE
Rosetta Stone 196 BCE			Roman general Pompey invades 63 BCE
		Octavian becomes Augustus Caesar in Rome 27 BCE	Herod the Great rules 37–4 BCE
			Pontius Pilate prefect of Judea 26–36 BCE
			Crucifixion of Jesus
			Letters of Paul ca. 50–60 CE
			Jerusalem destroyed by Rome 70 CE
			Gospels and other New Testament writings

Appendix C

New Testament Manuscripts Overview[1]

50–125 CE	First texts written down, copied, and distributed
172	Tatian Diatessaron, harmony of the gospels, in Syriac
200s–300s	Translations into Old Latin (North Africa) and Coptic (Egypt)
300s–400s	Great codices prepared: Sinaiticus, Alexandrinus, Vaticanus
384	Jerome completes Latin Vulgate version in Rome
400s	Syriac Peshitta translation prepared
500s	Codex Bezae prepared with Greek and Latin columns
6th c.	Gothic Bible translation prepared, Eastern Europe
10th–13th c.	Early Spanish, English, and French portions translated
1455	Gutenberg Bible in Latin published
1514	Complutensian Polyglot NT printed in Spain
1516	Greek edition of Erasmus published in Venice
1522	Martin Luther German translation published
1534	William Tyndale NT published
1569	Reina Spanish Bible version published
18th–19th c.	Discovery of ancient NT papyri fragments

---

1. Bible Odyssey, "History of the Text."

1881	Westcott and Hort Greek NT edition published; develop concept of manuscript families; rules evolve for text study
1898	Nestlé Greek edition published using Westcott-Hort
1966	United Bible Societies publish new eclectic Greek edition
2010	Society of Biblical Literature publishes Greek edition; uses Greek editions that draw from different text families

Appendix D

For Further Reading

OVERVIEW OF THE HISTORY OF THE BIBLE

John Barton, *A History of the Bible* (Viking, 2019)
Karen R. Keen, *The Word of a Humble God* (Eerdmans, 2022)
John D. Meade and Peter J. Gurry, *Scribes and Scripture* (Crossway, 2022)
Jaroslav Pelikan, *Whose Bible Is It? A History of the Scriptures through the Ages* (Viking, 2005)
Jacob L. Wright, *Why the Bible Began* (Cambridge, 2023).

BIBLE TRANSLATION

John Barton, *The Word: How We Translate the Bible and Why It Matters* (Basic, 2023)
Eugene A. Nida, *Fascinated by Languages* (J. Benjamins, 2003)
Ethel Emily Wallis, *God Speaks Navajo* (Wycliffe, 2000)

ANCIENT ISRAEL AND ARCHEOLOGY

Jodi Magness, *The Holy Land Revealed*, DVD, The Great Courses (Teaching Company, 2010)
Tremper Longman III, *Introducing the Old Testament: A Short Guide* (Zondervan Academic, 2012)

EXILE AND THE SECOND TEMPLE PERIOD

David A. DeSilva, *Introducing the Apocrypha: Message, Context, and Significance* (Baker Academic, 2018)

Malka Z. Simkovich, *Discovering Second Temple Literature: The Scriptures and Stories That Shaped Early Judaism* (University of Nebraska Press, Jewish Publication Society, 2018)

THE WORLD AND TIMES OF JESUS

Warren Carter, *Seven Events That Shaped the New Testament World* (Baker Academic, 2013)

C. D. Elledge, *The Bible and the Dead Sea Scrolls* (SBL, 2005).

Nijay K. Gupta, *A Beginner's Guide to New Testament Studies: Understanding Key Debates* (Baker Academic, 2020)

SPANISH AND ENGLISH BIBLES

Bruce M. Metzger, *The Bible in Translation: Ancient and English Versions* (Baker Academic, 2001)

Adam Nicholson, *God's Secretaries: The Making of the King James Bible* (HarperPerennial, 2005)

Mark Yoder, *Stronger Than Fire: The Spanish Bible Triumphs over the Inquisition* (TGS International, 2018)

HISTORY OF BIBLICAL INTERPRETATION

Craig Bartholomew, C. Stephen Evans, Mary Healy, and Murray Rae, eds., *"Behind" the Text: History and Biblical Interpretation* (Zondervan, 2003).

Pete Enns, "The History of Biblical Interpretation" (course), https://thebiblefornormalpeople.com/classes/interpretation/

William Yarchin, *History of Biblical Interpretation: A Reader*, (Baker Academic, 2011)

HISTORY, SCIENCE AND TEXT: MODERN QUESTIONS

William L. Burton, *Abba Isn't Daddy and Other Biblical Surprises* (Ave Maria, 2019)

Bart D. Ehrman, Craig A. Evans, and Robert B. Stewart. *Can We Trust the Bible on the Historical Jesus?* (Westminster John Knox, 2020)

Alister McGrath, *The Big Question: Why We Can't Stop Talking about Science, Faith, and God* (Saint Martin's, 2015)

FOR FURTHER READING

RECENT INTERPRETATIONAL ESSAYS

Craig G. Bartholomew, *Listening to Scripture: An Introduction to Interpreting the Bible* (Baker, 2023)
Daniel Cooperrider, *Speak with the Earth and It Will Teach You: A Field Guide to the Bible* (Pilgrim, 2022)
Miguel De La Torre, *Reading the Bible from the Margins* (Orbis, 2002)
Cheryl Bridges Johns, *Re-Enchanting the Text: Discovering the Bible as Sacred, Dangerous, and Mysterious* (Baker, 2023)
Esau McCaulley, *Reading while Black: African American Biblical Interpretation as an Exercise in Hope* (InterVarsity, 2020)
Gerald O. West, ed., *Reading Other-Wise: Socially Engaged Biblical Scholars Reading with Their Local Communities* (Society of Biblical Literature, 2007)
Deborah Spink Winters, ed., *Through Her Eyes: Bible Studies on Women in Scripture* (Judson, 2016)

Bibliography

Achenbach, Joel. "NASA Unveils First Images from James Webb Telescope." *Washington Post*, Jul 11, 2022. https://www.washingtonpost.com/science/2022/07/11/nasa-james-webb-space-telescope-images/.
Alison, James. "Brought to Life by Christ." *Christian Century* 137.18 (2002) 30–34. https://www.christiancentury.org/article/how-my-mind-has-changed/brought-life-christ.
Anderson, Amy, and Wendy Widder. *Textual Criticism of the Bible*. Bellingham, WA: Lexham, 2018.
Athanasius. *Letter 39*. In vol. 4 of The Nicene and Post-Nicene Fathers, Series 2. Edited by Philip Schaff. Repr., Peabody, MA: Hendrickson, 1994.
———. *The Life of Saint Antony*. Translated by Robert T. Meyer. Vol. 10 of Ancient Christian Writers. Westminster, MD: Newman, 1950.
Athas, George. "Setting the Record Straight: What Are We to Make of the Tel Dan Inscription?" *Journal of Semitic Studies* 51.2 (2006) 241–55.
Auerbach, Leo, ed. and trans. *Babylonian Talmud*. New York: Philosophical Library, 1944. https://sacred-texts.com/jud/bata/bataoo.htm.
Avenoza, Gemma, et al. "The Bible in Spanish and Catalan." In vol. 2 of *The New Cambridge History of the Bible*, 288–306. Cambridge: Cambridge University Press, 2012. DOI: 10.1017/CHOL9780521860062.
Avni, Gideon, and Jon Seligman. "Between the Temple Mount/Haram El-Sharif and the Holy Sepulchre: Archaeological Involvement in Jerusalem's Holy Places." *Journal of Mediteranean Archaeology* 19.2 (2006) 259–88. DOI: 10.1558/jmea.2006.v19i2.259.
Baecher, Claude. "Schleitheim Confession/Entente fraternelle entre quelques enfants de Dieu sur sept articles." In *L'Affaire Sattler*, 43–59. Méry-sur-Oise: Sator, 1990.
Barkay, Gabriel, et al. "The Challenges of Ketef Hinnom: Using Advanced Technologies to Reclaim the Earliest Biblical Texts and Their Context." *Near Eastern Archaeology* 66.4 (2003) 162–71.
Barton, John. *A History of the Bible: The Story of the World's Most Influential Book*. New York: Viking, 2019.
Bartsch, Carla. "Oral Style, Written Style, and Bible Translation." *Notes on Translation* 11.3 (1997) 41–48.
Bartusch, Mark W. "From Honor Challenge to False Prophecy: Rereading Jeremiah 28's Story of Prophetic Conflict in Light of Social-Science Models." *Currents in Theology and Mission* 36.6 (2009) 455–63.
Bauerschmidt, Frederick Christian. "God as Author: Thinking through a Metaphor." *Modern Theology* 31.4 (2015) 573–85. DOI: 10.1111/moth.12184.

Bellido, Emilio Monjo. "The Reformation in Spain in the Sixteenth Century (Part I)." *Southwestern Journal of Theology* 60.1 (2017) 15–31.

———. "The Reformation in Spain in the Sixteenth Century (Part II)." *Southwestern Journal of Theology* 60.1 (2017) 33–52.

Bennett, Harold V. "The Bible and Africentric Pentecostal Moral Decision-Making." *Journal of the Interdenominational Theological Center* 44 (2016) 1–17.

Ben-Tsiyon, Lurya, and Harold D. Halpern. "New Light on Unknown Prophets: 'The Lachish Letters.'" *Dor Le Dor* 1.4 (1973) 23–25.

Bible Odyssey. "A History of the Text of the New Testament." https://www.bibleodyssey.org/timeline-gallery/a-history-of-the-text-of-the-new-testament/.

Bonilla, Plutarco. "Cosas Olvidadas (o No Sabidas) Acerca de La Versión de Casiodoro de Reina, Luego Revisada Por Cipriano de Valera." *Revista Biblica* 57.3 (1995) 155–80.

Børresen, Kari Elisabeth, and Adriana Valerio, eds. *The High Middle Ages*. The Bible and Women Vol. 6.2. Atlanta: Society of Biblical Literature, 2015.

Bover y Oliver, José Maria. "La Vulgata en España." *Estudios Biblicos* 1.1 (1941) 11–40.

———. "La Vulgata en España." *Estudios Biblicos* 1.2 (1941) 167–85.

Boyarin, Daniel. *Border Lines: The Partition of Judaeo-Christianity*. Philadelphia: University of Pennsylvania Press, 2006.

———. *The Jewish Gospels: The Story of the Jewish Christ*. New York: New Press, 2012.

Bragt, Thieleman J. van. *The Bloodly Theater or Martyrs Mirror of the Defenseless Christians*. 5th ed. Translated by Joseph F. Sohm. Scottdale, PA: Herald, 1950.

Brehaut, Ernest. *An Encyclopedist of the Dark Ages: Isidore of Seville*. New York: Columbia University Press, 1912.

Brockman, Norbert C. "Crowther, Samuel Ajayi." *Dictionary of African Christian Biography*. https://dacb.org/stories/nigeria/crowther-samwel/.

Broom, Neil, and Robert Mann. "Creationism vs Evolution: But Not Creation vs Evolution." *Stimulus* 8.2 (2000) 16–22.

Broshi, Magan. "Excavations in the Chapel of St Vartan in the Holy Sepulchre." In *Ancient Churches Revealed*, edited by Yoram Tsafrir, 118–22. Washington, DC: Biblical Archaelogy Society, 1993.

Brown, Raymond E. *An Introduction to the New Testament*. New York: Doubleday, 1997.

Burton, William L. *Abba Isn't Daddy and Other Biblical Surprises*. Notre Dame, IN: Ave Maria, 2019.

Byrne, Ryan, and Bernadette McNary-Zak, eds. *Resurrecting the Brother of Jesus: The James Ossuary Controversy and the Quest for Religious Relics*. Chapel Hill: University of North Carolina Press, 2009.

Calvin, Jean. *Institutes of the Christian Religion*. Edited by John T. McNeill. Translated by Ford Lewis Battles. Library of Christian Classics 20–21. London: SCM, 1961.

Cannon, Katie Geneva. *Katie's Canon: Womanism and the Soul of the Black Community*. New York: Continuum, 1998.

Carasik, Michael, ed. and trans. *The Commentators Bible*. Melrose Park, PA: Jewish Publication Society, 2015.

Carey, William. *An Enquiry into the Obligations of Christians to Use Means for the Conversion of the Heathens*. London: Carey Kingsgate, 1792.

Carr, David M. *The Formation of the Hebrew Bible: A New Reconstruction*. Oxford: Oxford University Press, 2011.

———. "Orality, Textuality and Memory." In *Contextualizing Israel's Ancient Writings*, edited by Brian B. Schmidt, 161–74. Atlanta: Society of Biblical Literature, 2015.

———. "Rethinking the Materiality of Biblical Texts: From Source, Tradition and Redaction to a Scroll Approach." *Zeitschrift Für Die Alttestamentliche Wissenschaft* 132.4 (2020) 594–621. DOI: 10.1515/zaw-2020-4005.

Carter, Warren. *Seven Events That Shaped the New Testament World*. Grand Rapids: Baker Academic, 2013.

Cassian. *The Conferences*. Translated by Boniface Ramsey. Ancient Christian Writers 57. New York: Paulist, 1997.

"Catechism of the Catholic Church." https://www.vatican.va/archive/ENG0015/__PO.HTM.

Center for the Study of New Testament Manuscripts. "Manuscripts 101: Why Manuscripts?" https://www.csntm.org/manuscripts-101/.

Chapman, Stephen B. *The Law and the Prophets: A Study in Old Testament Canon Formation*. Grand Rapids: Baker Academic, 2020.

Charlesworth, James H., ed. *Old Testament Pseudepigrapha*. Vol. 2. Garden City, NY: Doubleday, 1985.

Clare of Assisi. "First Letter to Agnes of Prague." In *A Companion to Clare of Assisi: Life, Writings, and Spirituality*, by Joan Mueller, 261–63. Leiden: Brill, 2010.

Clifton-Soderstorm, Michelle. "Common Sense, Plain Sense, and Faithful Dissent: Evangelical Interpretation and the Ethics of Marriage Equality." *Journal of the Society of Christian Ethics* 37.1 (2017) 101–17.

Coakley, John W., and Andrea Sterk, eds. "Xian Inscription. Monument of the Church of the East at Xian." In *Readings in World Christian History: Earliest Christianity to 1453*, 243–47. Maryknoll: Orbis, 2004.

Combs, William W. "Erasmus and the Textus Receptus." *Detroit Baptist Seminary Journal* 1 (1996) 35–53.

Cooperrider, Daniel. *Speak with the Earth and It Will Teach You*. Cleveland, OH: Pilgrim, 2022.

Corbin-Reuschling, Wyndy. "'Trust and Obey': The Danger of Obedience as Duty in Evangelical Ethics." *Journal of the Society of Christian Ethics* 25.2 (2005) 59–77.

Cowley, A. E, ed. *Aramaic Papyri of the Fifth Century B.C.* Oxford: Clarendon, 1923. https://archive.org/details/aramaicpapyrioffooahikuoft/aramaicpapyrioffooahikuoft/page/n11/mode/2up.

Cuellar, Gregory. "Forgotten Forebears in the History of North American Biblical Scholarship." In *Latino/a Biblical Hermeneutics: Problemactics, Objectives, Strategies*, edited by Francisco Lozada Jr and Fernando F. Segovia, 121–32. Atlanta: Society of Biblical Literature, 2014.

"Cyrus Cylinder." *Livius*. Last modified October 12, 2020. https://www.livius.org/sources/content/cyrus-cylinder/.

Davis, Ellen F., and Richard B. Hays, eds. *The Art of Reading Scripture*. Grand Rapids: Eerdmans, 2003.

Dawes, Gregory W. *Introduction to the Bible*. Collegeville, MN: Liturgical, 2007.

DeSilva, David A. *Introducing the Apocrypha: Message, Context, and Significance*. Grand Rapids: Baker Academic, 2018.

Dever, William G. *My Nine Lives: Sixty Years in Israeli and Biblical Archaeology*. Atlanta: Society of Biblical Literature, 2020.

Dorfbauer, Lukas J. "Bethania, Bethara, or Bethabara: Fortunatianus of Aquileia and Origen's Commentary on John, with Particular Reference to John 1:28." *Commentaries, Catenae and Biblical Tradition: Papers from the Ninth Birmingham*

Colloquium on the Textual Criticism of the New Testament, in Association with the COMPAUL Project, 177–98. 2016.

Douglass, Frederick. "What To the Slave Is the Fourth of July?" *EDSITEment!* https://edsitement.neh.gov/student-activities/frederick-douglasss-what-slave-fourth-july.

Douglass, J. Robert. "Current Evangelical/Anabaptist Perspectives on the Inspiration of Scripture." *Brethren in Christ History and Life* 45.4 (2021) 173–98.

Durant, Will. *The Reformation: The Story of Civilization, Part VI*. New York: Simon and Schuster, 1957.

East, Brad. "Is Scripture a Gift? Reflections on the Divine-Ecclesial Provision of the Canon." *Religions* 13.10 (2022) 1–24. DOI: 10.3390/rel13100961.

Edwards, Dennis R. *What Is the Bible and How Do We Understand It?* Harrisonburg, VA: Herald, 2019.

Egeria. *Diary of a Pilgrimage*. Translated by George E. Gingras. New York: Newman, 1970.

Elledge, C. D. *The Bible and the Dead Sea Scrolls*. Atlanta: Society of Biblical Literature, 2005.

Eusebius. *The History of the Church: A New Translation*. Translated by Jeremy M. Schott. Berkeley: University of California Press, 2019.

Finkelstein, Israel, and Amihai Mazar. *The Quest for the Historical Israel: Debating Archaeology and the History of Early Israel*. Atlanta: Society of Biblical Literature, 2007.

Fisch, Yael. "The Origins of Oral Torah: A New Pauline Perspective." *Journal for the Study of Judaism in the Persian, Hellenistic, and Roman Period* 51.1 (2020) 43–66.

Fletcher, Richard. *The Conversion of Europe: From Paganism to Christianity 371–1386 AD*. United Kingdom: Fontana, 1998.

Francis of Assisi. *The Rule*. Ordo Fratrum Minorum. https://ofm.org/en/the-rule.html.

François, Wim. "Vernacular Bible Reading in Late Medieval and Early Modern Europe: The 'Catholic' Position Revisited." *Catholic Historical Review* 104.1 (2018) 23–56.

Frank, Georgia. *The Memory of the Eyes*. Berkeley: University of California Press, 2000.

Giberson, Karl. "Cosmos from Nothing." *Christian Century*, Jun 10, 2015.

González, Justo L. "Reading Ourselves in Spanish." *Apuntes* 17.1 (1997) 12–15.

———. *Santa Biblia: The Bible through Hispanic Eyes*. Nashville: Abingdon, 1996.

González, Ondina, and Justo González. *Nuestra Fe: A Latin American Church History Sourcebook*. Nashville: Abingdon, 2014.

Gorman, Michael J. *Elements of Biblical Exegesis: A Basic Guide for Students and Ministers*. 3rd ed. Grand Rapids: Baker Academic, 2020.

The Gospel Coalition. "Chicago Statement on Biblical Inerrancy." *Themelios* 4.3. https://www.thegospelcoalition.org/themelios/article/the-chicago-statement-on-biblical-inerrancy/.

Gray, James M. "The Inspiration of the Bible." In *The Fundamentals*, edited by R. A. Torrey et al. https://www.blueletterbible.org/Comm/torrey_ra/fundamentals/20.cfm.

Grey, Jacqueline. "Through the Looking Glass: Reflections on the Re-Evangelization of Europe through a Post-Colonial Reading of Isaiah 2:1–5." *Journal of the European Pentecostal Theological Association* 37.1 (2017) 28–39. DOI: 10.1080/18124461.2016.1267500.

Guder, Darrell L. *Called to Witness: Doing Missional Theology*. Grand Rapids: Eerdmans, 2015.

Hart, David Bentley, trans. *The New Testament: A Translation*. New Haven, CT: Yale University Press, 2017.

Havea, Jione. "Holy Baptism, Troubled Waters." *Liturgy* 34.2 (2019) 3–11. DOI: 10.1080/0458063X.2019.1604025.

Hays, Richard B. *Echoes of Scripture in the Letters of Paul*. Yale University Press, 1989.
Heater, Homer, Jr. "Once More, Jeremiah 10:4–10 Masoretic Text and the Septuagint." *Bibliotheca Sacra* 174.695 (2017) 301–11.
Heisey, Nancy R. "Women in Sixteenth-Century Anabaptism: Making a Difference." *Vox Benedictina* 9.1 (1992) 121–49.
Herodotus. *The History*. Translated by George Rawlinson. Great Books 6. Chicago: Encyclopedia Britannica, 1952.
Irenaeus. *Against Heresies*. Vol. 1 in *Ante-Nicene Fathers*. Edited by Alexander Robinson and James Donaldson. 10 vols. Repr., Peabody, MA: Hendrickson, 1994.
Irvin, Dale T., and Scott W. Sunquist. *History of the World Christian Movement*. Vol. 1. Maryknoll, NY: Orbis, 2001.
Jacobs, Louis. *A Concise Companion to the Jewish Religion*. New York: Oxford University Press, 1999. DOI: 10.1093/acref/9780192800886.001.0001.
Jerome. *Letter 57*. Vol. 6 of Nicene and Post-Nicene Fathers, Series 2. Edited by Philip Schaff. 14 vols. Repr., Peabody, MA: Hendrickson, 1994.
Josephus. *Flavius Josephus: Translation and Commentary*. Edited and translated by Steve Mason et al. 10 vols. Leiden: Brill, 1999–2023.
Julian of Norwich. *Showings*. Edited by Grace Warrack. London: Methuen, 1901. Repr., Project Gutenberg. https://www.gutenberg.org/files/52958/52958-h/52958-h.htm.
Keener, Craig S. *Christobiography: Memory, History, and the Reliability of the Gospels*. Grand Rapids: Eerdmans 2023.
Kirchhoffer, David G. "How Ecology Can Save the Life of Theology: A Philosophical Contribution to the Engagement of Ecology and Theology." In *Theology and Ecology across the Disciplines: On Care for Our Common Home*, edited by Celia Deane-Drummond and Rebecca Artinian-Kaiser, 53–63. London: T. & T. Clark, 2018.
Klaassen, Walter, ed. *Anabaptism in Outline*. Scottdale, PA: Herald, 1981.
Klein, F. A. "The Original Discovery of the Moabite Stone." *Palestine Exploration Fund Quarterly Statement* 2.6 (Mar–Jun 1870) 281–83. https://biblicalstudies.org.uk/articles_peq_01.php.
Knust, Jennifer Wright, and Tommy Wasserman. *To Cast the First Stone: The Transmission of a Gospel Story*. Princeton, NJ: Princeton University Press, 2019.
Koester, Helmut. *Ancient Christian Gospels*. Philadelphia: Trinity, 1990.
Laughlin, John C. H. "Archaeology." In *Anchor Bible Dictionary*, 1:232–47. Nashville: Abingdon, 2005.
Lausanne Movement. "Cape Town Commitment." https://lausanne.org/content/ctc/ctcommitment.
Letter of Aristeas. Translated by R. J. H. Shutt. In *The Old Testament Pseudepigrapha* 2, edited by James H. Charlesworth, 7–34. Garden City, NY: Doubleday, 1984.
Leuchter, Mark. "Jehoiakim and the Scribes: A Note on Jer 36,23." *Zeitschrift Für Die Alttestamentliche Wissenschaft* 127.2 (2015) 320–25. DOI: 10.1515/zaw-2015-0019.
Lévy, Carlos. "Philo of Alexandria." In *The Stanford Encyclopedia of Philosophy*, 2022. Edited by Edward N. Zalta and Uri Nodelman. https://plato.stanford.edu/archives/fall2022/entries/philo/.
Loewen, Jacob A. *The Bible in Cross-Cultural Perspective*. Pasadena, CA: William Carey, 2000.
Luther, Martin. *Prefaces to the New Testament*. Vol. 35 of *Luther's Works*. Philadelphia: Muhlenberg, 1960.
Magness, Jodi. *The Holy Land Revealed*. DVD. The Great Courses. 6 discs. Chantilly, VA: Teaching Company, 2010.

McKnight, Edgar V. *Reading the Bible Today: A Twenty-First Century Appreciation of Scripture*. Macon, GA: Smyth and Helwys, 2003.

McKnight, Scot. *The Second Testament: A New Translation*. Downers Grove, IL: IVP Academic, 2023.

Menno Simons. *The Complete Writings of Menno Simons*. Translated by Leonard Verduin. Edited by J. C. Wenger. Scottdale, PA: Herald, 1956.

Messmer, Andrew. "The Inspiration, Authority and Inerrancy of Scripture in the History of Christian Thought." *Evangelical Review of Theology* 45.4 (2021) 294–315.

Metzger, Bruce M. *The Bible in Translation: Ancient and English Versions*. Grand Rapids: Baker Academic, 2001.

———. *The Canon of the New Testament*. Oxford University Press, 1987.

Metzger, Bruce M., and Bart Ehrman. *The Text of the New Testament: Its Transmission, Corruption, and Restoration*. 3rd ed. Oxford University Press, 1992.

Millgram, Abraham E. *Jerusalem Curiosities*. Philadelphia: Jewish Publication Society, 1990.

Mitchell, Margaret M. "Origen and the Text-Critical Dilemma: An Illustration from One of His Newly Discovered Greek Homilies on the Psalms." *Biblical Research* 62 (2017) 61–82.

Moffett, Samuel Hugh. *A History of Christianity in Asia*. 2nd ed. Vol. 1. Maryknoll, NY: Orbis, 1998.

Moynihan, Colin. "He Taught Ancient Texts at Oxford. Now He Is Accused of Stealing Some." *New York Times*, Sep 27, 2021. https://www.nytimes.com/2021/09/24/arts/design/hobby-lobby-lawsuit-dirk-obbink.html.

Murray, Stuart. *Biblical Interpretation in the Anabaptist Tradition*. Kitchener, ON: Pandora, 2000.

Neff, David. "Meaning-Full Translations: The World's Most Influential Bible Translator, Eugene Nida, Is Weary of 'Word Worship.'" *Christianity Today*, Oct 7, 2002, 46–49. https://www.christianitytoday.com/ct/2002/october7/2.46.html.

Newton, Isaac. "Extract from 'General Scholium' from the Mathematical Principles of Natural Philosophy." 1729. *The Newton Project*. https://www.newtonproject.ox.ac.uk/view/texts/normalized/NATP00056.

Okoye, James Chukwuma. "Jesus and the Jesus Seminar." *New Theology Review* 20.2 (2007) 27–37.

Origen. *Homilies on Joshua*. Edited by Cynthia White. Translated by Barbara J. Bruce. Washington, DC: Catholic University of America Press, 2002.

———. *On First Principles*. Translated by G. W. Butterworth. Repr., Eugene, OR: Wipf & Stock, 2012.

Pelikan, Jaroslav. *Whose Bible Is It? A History of the Scriptures through the Ages*. New York: Viking, 2005.

Pérez Alonso, María Isabel. "Las Biblias Romanceadas Medievales o la Aventura de Traducir la 'Verdad Hebrayca' Al Castellano." *Helmántica* 62.188 (2011) 391–415.

Philo of Alexandria. *The Works of Philo: Complete and Unabridged*. Translated by C. D. Yonge. Peabody, MA: Hendrickson, 1993.

Pliny the Younger. *Complete Letters*. Translated by P. G. Walsh. Oxford: Oxford University Press, 2006.

Prieto Valladares, Jaime Adrián. "Historical Antecedents of Protestantism, the Beginnings of the Spread of the Bible in Independent Central America, and the Martyrdom of Juana Mendía (1783–1841)." *Journal of Latin American Theology* 6.2 (2011) 158–86.

BIBLIOGRAPHY

Puech, Émile. "James the Just, or Just James?: The 'James Ossuary' on Trial." *Bulletin of the Anglo-Israel Archaeological Society* 21 (2003) 45–53.

Rangel, Rawderson. "Breve História Da Tradução Da Bíblia Para O Espanhol." *Revista Batista Pioneira* 5.1 (2016) 183–202.

"Reform Judaism: The Tenets of Reform Judaism." *Jewish Virtual Library*. https://www.jewishvirtuallibrary.org/the-tenets-of-reform-judaism.

Reina, Casiodoro de. *A Declaration, or Confession of Faith: An English Translation of the 1577 Spanish Edition*. Translated by Steve Griffin and Andrew Messmer. Independently published, 2019.

Renan, Ernest. *Vie de Jésus*. Paris: Michel Lévy Frères, 1863. https://www.gutenberg.org/cache/epub/15113/pg15113-images.html.

Rienstra, Debra. *Refugia Faith: Seeking Hidden Shelters, Ordinary Wonders, and the Healing of the Earth*. Minneapolis: Fortress, 2022.

Ruden, Sarah, trans. *The Gospels: A New Translation*. New York: Modern Library, 2023.

Ruiz, Jean-Pierre, and Carmen M. Nanko-Fernández. "Dialogues in the Margins: The *Biblia de Alba* and the Future of Catholic-Jewish Understanding." In *Toward the Future: Essays on Catholic-Jewish Relations in Memory of Rabbi León Klenicki*, edited by Celia M. Deutsch et al., 35–51. New York: Paulist, 2013.

Russell, Norman, trans. *Lives of the Desert Fathers: The Historia monachorum in Aegypto*. Kalamazoo, MI: Cistercian, 1980.

Sabar, Ariel. "A Biblical Mystery at Oxford." *Atlantic*, Jun 2020. https://www.theatlantic.com/magazine/archive/2020/06/museum-of-the-bible-obbink-gospel-of-mark/610576/.

Sakenfeld, Katharine Doob, ed. *New Interpreter's Dictionary of the Bible (NIDB)*. 5 vols. Nashville: Abingdon, 2006–2009.

Sánchez-Cetina, Edesio. "Word of God, Word of the People: Translating the Bible in Post-Missionary Times." In *A History of Bible Translation*, edited by Philip A. Noss, 387–408. Rome: Edizioni de Storia e Letteratura, 2007.

Sánchez de Toca, Melchor. "A Never Ending Story: The Pontifical Commission on the Galileo Case. A Critical Review." In *The Inspiration of Astronomical Phenomena VI*, edited by E. M. Corsini, 99–108. San Francisco: Astronomical Society of the Pacific, 2011.

Sanneh, Lamin. *Translating the Message: The Missionary Impact on Culture*. Maryknoll, NY: Orbis, 1989.

Schmid, Konrad. "Who Wrote the Torah?" Institute for Advanced Study, 2018. https://www.ias.edu/ideas/2018/schmid-torah.

Serrano, Rafael A. *The History of the Spanish Bible: An Introduction*. 2nd ed. Independently published, 2017.

Shakespeare & Beyond. "Barbara Mowat on Editing Shakespeare." Folger Shakespeare Library, Nov 28, 2017. https://www.folger.edu/blogs/shakespeare-and-beyond/editing-shakespeare-barbara-mowat/.

Shapira, Dan D. Y. "Our Daily Bread Is at Risk: The Term Rōzīq/g as Vorlage for Ἐπιούσιος in Lord's Prayer." *Verbum Vitae* 40.4 (2022) 1097–101. DOI: 10.31743/vv.14470.

Smith, Julie Ann. "'My Lord's Native Land': Mapping the Christian Holy Land." *Church History* 76.1 (2007) 1–31.

Smith, Mark S. "God Male and Female in the Old Testament: Yahweh and His 'Asherah.'" *Theological Studies* 48.2 (1987) 333–40.

Smith, Mitzi J. "A Womanist Activist Approach to Biblical Interpretation and Justice." *Touchstone* 40.1 (2022) 37–45.

BIBLIOGRAPHY

Snyder, C. Arnold. *Anabaptist History and Theology.* Kitchener, ON: Pandora, 1997.

———. *Following in the Footsteps of Christ: The Anabaptist Tradition.* Maryknoll, NY: Orbis, 2004.

Society of Biblical Literature. "The Hebrew Bible: A Critical Edition." https://www.sbl-site.org/publications/Books_HBCE.aspx.

Suetonius. *Lives of the Caesars.* Translated by Catherine Edwards. Oxford: Oxford University Press.

Tertullian. *On Idolatry.* In vol. 3 of The Ante-Nicene Fathers. Edited by Alexander Roberts and James Donaldson. Repr., Peabody, MA: Hendrickson, 1994.

Tidmore, Hollis D. "Progressive Creationism versus Theistic Evolution as a Christian Worldview." *Faith and Mission* 17.3 (2000) 79–88.

Ulrich, Eugene. *Dead Sea Scrolls and the Developmental Composition of the Bible.* Leiden: Brill, 2015.

———. "Our Sharper Focus on the Bible and Theology Thanks to the Dead Sea Scrolls." *Catholic Biblical Quarterly* 66.1 (2004) 1–24.

Voth, Esteban. "Hacia una Ética de Liberación para la Traducción Bíblica." *Revista Pistis & Praxis* 8.1 (2016) 33–54. DOI: 10.7213/revistapistispraxis.08.001.ds02.

Wallis, Ethel Emily. *God Speaks Navajo.* Wycliffe, 2000.

Ward, Mark L. "Which Textus Receptus? A Critique of Confessional Bibliology." *Detroit Baptist Seminary Journal* 25 (2020) 51–77.

Waterworth, J., ed. and trans. *The Canons and Decrees of the Sacred and Oecumenical Council of Trent.* London: C. Dolman, 1848.

West, Gerald O. "Reading the Bible with the Marginalised: The Value/s of Contextual Bible Reading." *Stellenbosch Theological Journal* 1.2 (2015) 235–61. DOI: 10.17570/stj.2015.v1n2.a11.

Westcott, B. F., ed. "Codex Canonum Ecclesiae Africanae." In *A General Survey of the History of the New Testament Canon*, 439–42. 6th ed. Repr., Eugene, OR: Wipf & Stock, 2005.

Wikipedia. "Clergy Letter Project." Last updated February 11, 2023. https://en.wikipedia.org/wiki/Clergy_Letter_Project.

Wolf, Kenneth Baxter. "*Convivencia* in Medieval Spain: The Brief History of an Idea." *Religion Compass* 3.1 (2009). DOI: 10.1111/j.1749-8171.2008.00119.x.

Wolters, Albert M. "Anthrōpoi Eudokias (Luke 2:14) and 'Nšy Rṣwn (4Q416)." *Journal of Biblical Literature* 113.2 (1994) 291–92.

Wood, Gabe. "How Many People Speak Spanish? A Full Breakdown by Country." Rosetta Stone, May 11, 2023. https://blog.rosettastone.com/how-many-people-speak-spanish-a-full-breakdown-by-country/.

Younger, K. Lawson, Jr. "The Fall of Samaria in Light of Recent Research." *Catholic Biblical Quarterly* 61.3 (1999) 461–82.

Young, Robin Darling. "The Lady Advances: The Voices of Women in Early Christianity." *Journal of Early Christian Studies* (2023) 263–82.

Zogbo, Lynell. "Issues in Bible Translation in Africa." *Review & Expositor* 108.2 (2011) 279–96.

www.ingramcontent.com/pod-product-compliance
Lightning Source LLC
Chambersburg PA
CBHW051108160426
43193CB00010B/1363